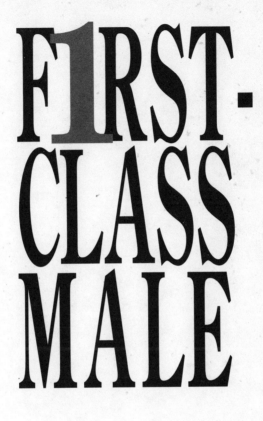

F1RST-CLASS MALE

The Christian man's role in today's world

LEN McMILLAN

MARVIN WRAY

REVIEW AND HERALD® PUBLISHING ASSOCIATION
HAGERSTOWN, MD 21740

The author assumes full responsibility for the accuracy of all facts and quotations as cited in this book.

Texts credited to NIV are from the *Holy Bible, New International Version.* Copyright © 1973, 1978, 1984, International Bible Society. Used by permission of Zondervan Bible Publishers.

Texts credited to NKJV are from The New King James Version. Copyright © 1979, 1980, 1982, Thomas Nelson, Inc., Publishers.

Bible texts credited to RSV are from the Revised Standard Version of the Bible, copyright © 1946, 1952, 1971, by the Division of Christian Education of the National Council of the Churches of Christ in the U.S.A. Used by permission.

Verses marked TLB are taken from *The Living Bible*, copyright © 1971 by Tyndale House Publishers, Wheaton, Ill. Used by permission.

This book was
Edited by Richard W. Coffen
Designed by Patricia S. Wegh
Cover design by Helcio Deslandes
Typeset: Times 11/13

PRINTED IN U.S.A.

99 98 97 96 95 94   5 4 3 2

Library of Congress Cataloging in Publication Data
McMillan, Len D., 1938-
    First class male: a Christian man's role in today's world/Len McMillan, Marvin Wray.
            p.   cm.
    1. Men (Christian theology)   2. Men—United States—Life skills guides.
I. Wray, Marvin.   II. Title.
BT703.5.M37   1994
261.8'3431—dc20
                                                              94-2254
                                                              CIP

ISBN 0-8280-0786-1

Contents

Preface

The International Labor Organization, a United Nations agency, recently did a survey that asked women around the world how much help men give them with the housework. According to the results, most women think the average man is doing a splendid job.

I'm joking, of course. Actually the women said that in terms of sharing the housework burden, having a man around the house is like having a 180-pound lint ball permanently sitting on the sofa, systematically punching the buttons on the TV remote control, and periodically generating dirty underwear and other unsavory items.

Such criticism is nothing new to the average male. After all, that's all part of being a man. Somebody is always surveying women about men, and men always come out looking bad. Why? It's because the pollsters are asking women rather than men! If you really want to get some factual information about men, whom should you ask? Other men, of course!

Or perhaps the problem has to do with the survey questions. If we changed the questions, perhaps men would appear in a more positive light. For example:

• Which gender, on the average, is more likely to demonstrate the patience and perseverance necessary to teach a small child how to spit?

• In the event of a family emergency, which gender is most likely to be able to remember—calmly and without panic—what position Clarence "Choo Choo" Coleman played?

If surveys contained questions like these, men would get a better grade, even from women. But surveys never ask questions like that. Instead, they always ask about female-oriented qualities, such as maturity, sensitivity, communication, commitment, facility of remembering the names of the children, ability to recall accurately an anniversary date, etc. Such questions completely ignore the male world.

But when did you last see a survey asking questions about sensitive male issues? Probably never. Instead, you saw questions about housework and other feminine pursuits. Men's poor showing in the surveys isn't really their fault. Men have been conditioned by thousands of years of culture to be the hunter-gatherer. Therefore, most men are better suited for more aggressive, physical, strenuous activities, such as golf.

Besides, on those rare occasions when a man does attempt to help out with some household responsibility, such as getting the kids dressed for school, he often discovers that his wife has established a lot of picky, technical rules—for instance, socks must match. And there's other trivia. Tired of being corrected, he eventually gives up and retreats to the golf course, where he can aggressively vent his frustration with his driver.

Another problem is that TV commercials promoting housework-type products are always aimed at women. The white tornado and the man from Glad were never actually cleaning the toilet bowl; they were merely lounging around in the bathroom. Television needs to produce commercials that will make housework appealing to guys. Using a toilet plunger to rescue a damsel in distress would be much more appealing to the male macho image.

Although it is true that men need to be more sensitive to the opposite sex, at the same time women need to become more aware of an important fact that is often overlooked amid the endless day-to-day hassles involved in running a household: "Choo Choo" Coleman was a catcher.

CHAPTER 1

What Is a Man?

Walking home along the railroad tracks, a group of school-boys started playing chicken with oncoming trains. The biggest boy, O.T., always won at this particular game even though he was failing in school. One afternoon he charged a boxcar from the side, stopping just short of throwing himself between the wheels. Impressed with his daring, the others all conceded that O.T. was the bravest in their group.

Later, as the boys skipped stones across a farmer's pond, they debated whether or not someone could dive under a moving boxcar, stay put for a count of 10, and then scramble out the other side. One boy, Roger, thought it could be done.

"I dare you," O.T. taunted.

No words are more challenging to a 12-year-old boy. In fact, it never occurred to Roger that he really had a choice. "I accept!" Roger replied with false confidence. After all, it was a *dare*!

Roger scouted the railroad tracks and trains every spare moment during the next two weeks. He memorized the construction of box-cars and carefully measured the clearance beneath their axles. In bed at night he would visualize an imaginary freight train and run along-side it. Early each morning he went to the railroad tracks to master a shallow headfirst dive with a simple half-twist. Landing on his back, he would count to 10 and then lock both hands on the rail to his left and heave himself over and out from under the imaginary train.

Finally, on a designated day, O.T. and three other eighth graders accompanied Roger to the railroad tracks, just below the hill that backed up to the lumberyard. The tracks followed a low bed there and opened to a straight, slightly uphill, climb for about a half mile. Roger knelt on one knee beside the track. O.T. came to his side, and Roger gave him his wallet and house key. In silence O.T. and the others made their way back to the top of the hill to watch.

Roger felt the tracks vibrating before he saw the train coming around the bend. The engineer blew the whistle and waved at him to back away from the track. The train was laboring to climb the hill when Roger started to run alongside the boxcars. They were going faster than he had anticipated, but he quickly began keeping pace with them. Over his shoulder he spotted one boxcar

We must first define what it means to be a man.

with a white mountain goat painted on its side. *That's the one!* he thought. Running faster to keep pace with the white mountain goat, he dipped his shoulder and dived beneath the train.

Boxcars shook the earth like a stampeding herd of cattle thundering overhead. A voice inside Roger kept repeating, *Watch the axles, count to 10, and look to your left for daylight.* He couldn't count and couldn't see daylight. Overhead a kaleidoscope of colors changed from brown to red to black to red again. Finally, Roger ripped his hands free, forced them to the rail, and in one convulsive jerk, threw himself into the blue light.

Stunned, he lay there beside the tracks until there was no more noise. As the train faded away in the distance Roger sat up. O.T. led a charge down the hill as all the boys twirled their fists in the air in triumphal joy. Roger sat still beside the tracks and pulled his knees tight against his chest to cover the wetness across the front of his corduroy pants.

Why? Why does a male find it necessary to risk his life on a dare? Why do males take risks? Why are most wars fought by men? Why do males have a competitive spirit? Why is saving face sometimes viewed as more important than saving life? Why do men become breadwinners, star athletes, computer junkies, or workaholics? To answer these questions, we must define what it means to be a man.

The Typical Male

According to a definition found in *Men's Health* (February

1991) the typical adult male:

• thinks about sex every 15 minutes until age 40, when such thoughts occur only once every half hour. He makes 3 million sperm every hour and has sex 2.5 times per week.

• produces about 25 feet of hair in his lifetime. One out of five will go bald in his 20s, and the same number will retain a full head of hair until his dying day.

• will take in enough air during his lifetime to fill two blimps the size of the *Hindenburg*.

• retains about 60 percent of his body weight in water and will produce up to a half gallon of sweat daily. He prefers a shower rather than a bath to remove his perspiration, and one out of three will sing while showering.

• has a heart that pumps about 50 million gallons of blood and beats around 2.5 billion times during his lifetime.

• walks 1,250 miles per year, and even though he is not the fastest animal on earth, he can outrun any other species for long distances.

• consumes 2,400 calories per day, and his body is so efficient that if he ran on gasoline, he'd get 900 miles per gallon.

• has a brain that weighs almost three pounds. (Some employers or spouses would suggest that is an optimistic estimate at best.)

• sleeps 54.8 hours per week.

• falls in love an average of six times during his lifetime. Is married and would marry his spouse again.

• cries about once a month, approximately one fourth as often as a woman, and he usually tries to hide it.

• eats his corn on the cob in circles rather than straight across.

• does not know his cholesterol count (approximately 211) and won't go to the doctor unless it is an emergency.

• thinks he looks just fine in the nude, no matter what his body weight.

• will not stop to ask for directions when he's in a car.

• follows pro football but lets his wife buy all his underwear.

• lives eight years less than the typical woman, even though more males are conceived than females.
• 125 male embryos are conceived for every 100 females.
• 105 baby boys are born for every 100 females.
• There are 100 men age 18 for every 100 females.
• There are 68 men aged 65 or older for every 100 females.
• There are 44 men aged 85 or older for every 100 females.

The Male Movement

Men share a diverse legacy in America. Early settlers in the Northeast were basically farmers and arrived in New England during the 1600s. Extremely proud of their introversion and ability to withstand pain, New England males were willing to sit on wooden benches without backs through three services in an unheated church.

Southern males shared a concept of expansion, motherhood, and a cavalier attitude. No matter what, the chivalrous Southern male protected his mother and was bound to her with an invisible cord throughout his life.

Males raised in the East became entrepreneurs and couldn't seem to get enough to satisfy their longing for material goods. Most railroad and industrial millionaires were from the East.

Western males were raised to be a reckless, violent breed with an I-will-do-without attitude.

One writer summed it up well: "We like to think of masculinity as biologically determined, but most of

"We like to think of masculinity as biologically determined, but most of its origins are cultural and historical."

its origins are cultural and historical and so vary from time to time and place to place. It doesn't exist just in the mind of an individual man; it's a view of life shared by other men" (*Psychology Today*, January/February 1992, p. 79).

During the brief half century of my lifetime, I have seen remarkable changes in the definition of manhood. The *fifties* male arrived at work early and worked late. He labored responsibly for one company throughout his working years and retired with a gold watch and little else. He viewed himself as the breadwinner and faithfully supported his wife and children. He admired discipline, especially in himself. He appreciated women's bodies but did not value their inner being. Capable of fixing anything, he enjoyed a feeling of superiority when women and children came to him for assistance. He was aggressive, liked football, stuck up for the U.S., and never cried. He needed an enemy to make him feel alive, and the cold war provided a convenient reality check on his existence.

During the *sixties* men were subjected to the horrors of Vietnam. For some it meant fleeing to Canada to avoid the draft. For others it was their patriotic duty—at least until they became aware of the political quagmire that manifested itself in a war they were never meant to win. If manhood meant fighting in Vietnam, did they want any part of it? During this time, the feminist movement encouraged men to actually look at women as second-class citizens without true equality in society. As men began to examine the feminist claims, they began to discover their feminine side. The sixties male began a transition that continues to the present.

The Vietnam War left its mark of waste and violence on the *seventies* male. The feminist movement caused him to examine his *feminine* side. He was sometimes viewed as a *soft* male, interested in saving the earth and preventing wars, rather than abusing the earth and killing others. He had a gentle attitude toward life that some would refer to as hippie-ish. Basically unhappy and confused, he usually married a strong woman who radiated newfound positive energy as feminism made her more assertive.

The *eighties* male has been referred to by some as the *lite* man. Less fat, more tender, tastefully dressed, no body odor, a man for all microwaves. Women chewed on him for a decade, but eventually spit him out. There was something missing. A dynamic of maleness that was both attractive and violent in previous males had been lost. Women were being freed from the bondage of stereotypes and cultural adaptation, but men were lagging behind in their own discoveries.

Now the *nineties* male is making preparations to enter the twenty-first century. Masculinity has become a problem for both males and females. The qualities that were useful in protecting primitive society from mastodons and saber-toothed tigers have few practical functions today. Look at any major metropolitan area, and you see cities full of men stomping around, flexing their muscles, and growling manly noises at one another in our modern jungles. Spouse and child abuse is a national epidemic.

Men are not only behind in cultural reform but also in biological understanding. In alarming numbers, men drink themselves sick, take drugs, work themselves to death, run away from home in midlife, and kill others. Though still alive enough to be aware of what it feels like to be a man, they often feel isolated from other men and peripheral to their family. Many trudge along, wasting their lives in meaningless work, with very little sense of where they are going or where they have been.

Men of the fifties have little empathy with or understanding of the nineties male. Whereas the fifties male was seen as the hard-driving, breadwinning, dominating, sometimes vulgar king of his castle, the nineties male is more flexible, with emphasis on being a good, supportive marriage partner and parent with more refined manners and a tendency to show emotions other than anger. The fifties male was demanding and aggressive in both his emotional and sexual desires. The nineties male tends to be assertive rather than aggressive and seeks to be a nurturing lover to his mate. The fifties male viewed his spiritual life in terms of absolutes—immobile dogma—that were viewed as absolute *truth*. The nineties male is more paradoxical and relates better to direct experience rather than dogma or inflexible *truths*. This may be the first time in history when two adult generations living at the same time share such widely divergent views of manhood. It is almost as though spaceships from two alien planets have crash-landed here on earth, leaving the survivors to define the future of men.

Some have questioned whether there really is a men's movement in the nineties. The answer is yes and no (a typical paradoxical nineties reply). While the women's movement of the past few decades has touched the lives of

One survey indicates that 51 percent of women and 55 percent of men think the women's movement has made things more difficult for men.

millions, both men and women, the men's movement has touched only a few thousand.

While the women's movement responded enthusiastically to rectifying centuries-old injustices, the men's movement has not experienced such urgency, because men were in a position of power. Women felt a passion to change the system that many men supported. Anytime you lose power, it is a difficult adjustment. It is easy to understand male reluctance to change a system that gave them complete control.

In the midst of this male confusion, women have been sending mixed signals concerning masculinity. Manhood was understood by all a few decades ago, but now its definition seems to change from one day to the next. Some women want a husband to be a typical hardworking breadwinner who is also sensitive to her needs and feelings. However, she may feel insecure when he talks about being a sensitive father or a househusband.

Dating used to be a simple procedure: men made the first move after being coyly encouraged by the female. Now it is a scene of chaos for some men. For example, who picks up the check after a dinner date? Do you split the cost, since both are probably employed? Do you alternate picking up the check? Does the man pay the check and the woman repay him in private? Or does the man still pick up the check? It seems like the spirit of mothers and grand-mothers often takes control of nineties females as soon as the check arrives. Suddenly their arms become paralyzed, and try as they will, they just can't seem to reach out for that piece of paper.

Manhood in America has been unthinkingly defined as "be a man!" What that definition means to many is to be stupid—be un-feeling—be obedient and a good soldier. It is interesting how girls have traditionally been urged to please adults with a kind of coquet-tishness, whereas boys are encouraged to behave like monkeys to-ward each other, and we comment, "Boys will be boys!" At a young age, even nineties females learn how to become women in a subtle power game in which they quickly learn to be sexually indispensable, socially decorative, and always alert to a man's sense of inadequacy. *Femininity implies needing a man as witness and seducer, but mas-culinity celebrates the exclusive company of men* (Phyllis Chesler, *About Men*, p. 236). Most men are not taught how to relate to women, but instead are indoctrinated with the superiority of males.

It is difficult to imagine any concept of manliness that does not belittle women, and it begins at an early age. By words and example, boys are taught—even by their mothers—the superiority of mas-culinity. This superiority is then focused in one area, his ability to at-tract women. The average man feels fully masculine only if he can attract a woman, thus granting her terrifying power over him. Not only must he win her, but he must also satisfy her. A woman can utterly

Manhood was understood by all a few decades ago, but now its definition seems to change from one day to the next.

deflate a man by refusing to be aroused sexually or by refusing to be satisfied. Men are terrified by a woman's anger, because it returns him to his childhood with Mom (*Psychology Today*, January/February 1992, p. 82).

The basic quest for manliness is too often a right-wing, puritani-
cal, cowardly, neurotic quest fueled largely by an unreasonable fear
of women. It is not coincidental that the first masculinity/femininity
test was developed and published in 1936 . . . right in the midst of the
Great Depression. The Depression undermined the most important
basis of a man's identity—his ability to work and support his family
(*Psychology Today*, July 1987, p. 51). It is important to note that it is
not necessary to bash femininity in order to define masculinity.
Rather than looking for areas of inferior-superior comparison, it is
more profitable to look at differences as complementing an overall
plan implemented by God at Creation. God did not create man superior and woman inferior (see Gen. 1, 2). It was sin that created the
first power struggle between male and female (Gen. 3), and we have
been reaping the consequences ever since.

There seem to be three basic categories of males currently interested in a men's movement. *Pro-feminists* engage in consciousness-
raising groups and promote women's rights and sex roles. Phil
Donahue is an example of this group of males. While this group is
bringing male support to the women's movement, it has done little
in the way of defining manhood. One author comments: "We have
to ask ourselves, 'Is this new liberated male in reality only a femi-
nized male, who in showing greater openness of feelings has become
more like a woman?'" (Robert Hicks, *Uneasy Manhood: The Quest
for Self-understanding*, p. 38). Is masculinity merely a redefined
femininity?

Another part of the men's movement is called the *no-guilt* group.
It tells men not to feel guilty about their sex roles with women.
These men point out that both males and females are victims of sex
roles and social changes. Men belonging to the conservative right
have mounted a major backlash against the no-guilt and pro-feminist
males, using the Bible to prove male superiority. Those who refuse
to accept their views of Scripture are often written off as apostates or
nonbelievers. Like the fifties male, the men on the conservative right
are comfortable only with dogma and absolutes.

Herb Goldberg, author of *The New Male*, is quoted as saying: "What has been commonly described as 'men's lib' is not liberation at all, but merely accommodation to women's changes. What this means is that once again he is playing daddy, only this time, unlike in the traditional relationship where he got nurturance and support, the payoffs are almost nonexistent" (quoted in Anthony Astrachan, *How Men Feel: Their Response to Women's Demands for Equality and Power*, p. 305). The no-guilt males seek to understand how culture has formed stereotypes and how both men and women can be freed from their molds.

A third group in the men's movement is concerned with *divorce and child custody*. It seeks to overcome the advantages women currently have in custody suits as well as alimony payments. The group is militant and angry. It takes great joy in female celebrities being sued by their former spouses for support. What these men tend to ignore is that few men actually pay child support or alimony. It is one thing to demand justice in our legal system, but we must also demand honor among men. For many men a divorce prompts them to hide their earnings—and sometimes even their identity—so that they do not have to pay. This lack of responsibility has angered the women's movement and shows little compassion for dependent children who have neither a father nor food.

The question is no longer Have men changed? The answer to that is a resounding yes! Now we must concern ourselves with how much change is desirable? In what ways should men change? And what end product do we desire? We should not attempt to remake ourselves into Ken and Barbie dolls with interchangeable parts. That is the mistake of some male and female movements. Rather, let's begin to understand and celebrate male-female differences as designed by God.

Understanding the male role in our society is confusing at best. "Our culture has largely rejected the image of manhood that we cut our teeth on, and the one that on an intellectual level we may admit is Victorian or bigoted" (Hicks, p. 33). How can the new man get in touch with true male feelings without feeling guilt or shame? Men often view feelings as moral issues that need to be judged. It is difficult for the typical male to accept feelings as barometers of high and low pressure areas without assigning guilt to their presence. Feelings need to be listened to, understood, and considered important if men are to throw off the male myth. One thing that both men and women have in

We should not attempt to remake ourselves into Ken and Barbie dolls with interchangeable parts. That is the mistake of some male and female movements. Rather, let's begin to understand and celebrate male-female differences as designed by God.

common is the need to love and be loved. Perhaps that is our point of contact and where the two sexes need to concentrate their greatest efforts and understanding.

Most males find it difficult to develop a sense of self-worth apart from their employment or career. Unlike women, who have been able to succeed at life without glorious careers to bolster their self-esteem, men are just beginning to learn these lessons. I read where one businessman was feeling harassed and discouraged from overwork. Fearing burnout, he took his problem to a counselor, who immediately urged him to do less work. "Furthermore," the counselor continued, "I want you to spend one hour each week in the cemetery."

"What on earth do you want me to do that for?" the man replied incredulously. "What should I do in a cemetery?"

"Not much," the counselor replied. "Take it easy, and look around. Get acquainted with some of the men already in there, and remember that they didn't finish their work either."

Unfortunately, many men use work to prove something to themselves, to their fathers, or to early mentors about their own value as a man. When two males are introduced, the most common second question is "What do you do?" which immediately follows "How do you do?"

What men need is a clear understanding of what is expected of them as a male. Perhaps a generally accepted New Male Manifesto is a place to begin.

1. Masculinity is life-affirming and life-supporting. Male sexuality generates life, and the male body also needs to be nurtured and protected.

2. Male value is not measured by what a man produces—rather by what he is.

3. Men do not need to become like women to find their complete self.

4. Masculinity does not require denial of our true feelings.

5. Men can be brothers as well as competitors.

6. Fatherhood is honorable and an essential part of family life.

7. Men and women can be equal partners.

Obviously this manifesto is easier read than lived. Many forces are currently trying to redefine the *new man* as we enter the next century. Feminists want gender-neutral terminology that no longer refers to male or female. Gays rage against heterosexuality and in their attempt to gain equal rights want to redefine manhood. Movies and television project men as bunglers or superheroes. Books and periodicals criticize men for not spending enough time with their families. Wives criticize men for not doing their fair share of work at home and for being insensitive. Corporations are

What men need is a clear understanding of what is expected of them as a male.

demanding more dedication and loyalty, leaving little time for anything else in a man's life.

These and other forces are in the process of shaping the new man. Unfortunately, most of the shaping is coming from special-interest groups, while the majority of males are having little impact upon defining manhood for the twenty-first century. *Psychology Today* polled readers to determine the ideal man (November 1989, pp. 54-60). Those completing the survey defined manhood in four categories. The *inferior man* was seen as cynical and materialistic, living by the creed that he who dies with the most toys wins. The *average man* doesn't want to rock the boat and may be either liberal or conservative. The *good man* views his most important duty as his family. He places a high value on responsibility and duty. He lives by the creed that God helps those who help themselves.

The highest level of masculinity was referred to as the *ideal man*. He leaves the world a better place than he found it; is receptive and responsive to the initiatives of others; and has a strong intellectual, moral, or physical presence. He pays attention to his diet, exercise, and health. He expresses feelings of sadness and stops often to wonder, appreciate, and dream. He follows an inner authority or "still small voice." He is even-tempered, moderate, and easy to be with. Nonjudgmental, he willingly accepts help from others. In fact, the type A personality ranked near the bottom of the ideal list.

The number one ideal man listed by both men and women was Jesus! It is interesting, considering the current controversy over manhood, that the number two choice for both sexes was Gandhi. Adolf Hitler was voted the most inferior man, whereas Ronald Reagan was the only man to make all four lists (ideal, good, average, and inferior).

Regardless of surveys or categories, who is a *real man* today? Is it the macho and unfeeling Rambo, or the sensitive and humorous Hawkeye Pierce? Actually, there is only one man who ever lived exactly as God created us to live. If we are going to look for role models to help define the new man, we can't do better than God's own Son. Our attempt to develop into a real man apart from a relationship with our Creator is doomed to failure.

A great violinist once visited Houston, Texas, to hold a concert. The newspapers used most of their available space to describe his original, and extremely valuable, Stradivarius violin. On the morning of the concert, the papers actually carried a picture of the great instrument that he would use.

That night the hall filled with people, and the violinist played extremely well. As he finished, applause thundered from every part of the concert hall. After it subsided, he carefully laid down his bow and carried a chair out to center stage. Raising the violin over his head with both hands, he smashed it across the back of the chair. It splintered into a thousand pieces.

The audience gasped and sat stunned. Coming back to the microphone, he said, "I read in this morning's paper how great my violin was. So I walked down the street and found a pawnshop. For $10 I bought a cheap violin. I put new strings on it, and that's the violin I played this evening, the smashed one. I wanted to demonstrate for you that it isn't my violin that counts most. It's the hands that hold the violin."

Likewise, living as a Christian male depends less on the instrument (body) and more on the One who holds us. Manhood is not found in physical abilities, emotional outbursts of anger, dominating behavior, personality and charisma, talent, intelligence, performance, or profession. Real manhood is found in the *inner man*, evidenced by moral character, ethical firmness, and quality of life.

It has been said, "The cheaper the merchandise, the higher the gloss!" In the furniture industry the quality of inferior material is often hidden by a high gloss. Furniture made from inferior woods generally has layers of lacquer or paint applied to camouflage the poor quality. However, furniture made from quality wood needs only oil or a soft polish to bring out its inner beauty. Men who are of inferior quality often try to hide their imperfections by becoming workaholics or dominating competitors. This glosses over any inner man that might try to peek through the layers of masks and cultural expectations imposed by society and self.

A real man possesses self-awareness and courage. He critically examines why he believes the things he believes, feels the way he feels, and values the things he does. He is constantly searching and knows his own heart. He is filled with the Holy Spirit and rejoices in both his strengths and those of others. A real man is not afraid to admit when he is wrong and takes a realistic view of his God-given talents and cultivated abilities.

> *A real man possesses self-awareness and courage. He critically examines why he believes the things he believes, feels the way he feels, and values the things he does.*

George was *not* a Mr. Fixit! If anything, he was a Mr. Klutz when it came to home and auto repairs. However, his wife, Carol, grew up in a home where men fixed everything. So George felt that he must carry on the male tradition. He bought a whole library of how-to books that could transform him into a "real" man.

One morning his 12-year-old Volkswagen van wouldn't start. George decided to fix the problem. Realizing the battery was dead, he got out his books and began. In order to take off the generator, which he surmised was the problem, he had to remove the fan and carburetor. His wife encouraged him by saying, "Just think how good you're going to feel when you get it working again." George tried to keep a positive attitude, but there was nothing good about skinned knuckles, a hammered thumb, and a self-inflicted groin injury he had sustained trying to unfreeze a rusted bolt.

It took him three days to track down the parts, install a rebuilt generator, and replace the fan and carburetor. His male ego responded joyfully when the 46-horsepower engine roared to life. Happy but sore, he accepted the accolades from his wife. The next morning the battery was dead again. This time George called a tow truck. The tow truck operator arrived with a long pair of jumper cables and lifted the cover on the battery box. "Whoever sold you this generator must have taken you for a fool," the man remarked as he wiggled the battery cables. "All you needed was to clean the battery posts."

That night George rescinded his earlier pledge to become a fixer. He confessed to Carol that he was not a fixer, never would be a fixer, and did not even want to become a fixer. If that's what it took to be a man, he guessed he didn't measure up.

Carol assured George that she knew all along he couldn't fix things

> *Another aspect of a real man is his ability to make—and keep— commitments. Real men are not afraid to commit publicly or privately, and they always keep their word.*

and that she encouraged him only because he thought it so important in his role as a man. She assured George that she still loved him, and later when the turntable on the stereo quit turning, she got out his toolbox and made the repairs herself.

Another aspect of a real man is his ability to make—and keep— commitments. Real men are not afraid to commit publicly or privately, and they always keep their word. Not like the big, burly-looking man who was moved by a sermon one week and on his way out of church pledged, "Pastor, you really inspired me with your sermon on the Ten Commandments. I've already made up my mind that starting today I'm going to keep one commandment a week until I get through all 10."

Real men are candid and not afraid to face the truth. They are teachable and willing to listen as well as face the consequences of their actions. Real men care about their family, neighbors, community, church, nation, and the world in which they live. They become involved in the lives of others and give of their time and resources.

Real men believe in God and seek to know Him both as their Creator and Friend. They live by their beliefs and are willing to follow the path God creates for them, even if it means changing direction. Real men are worthy of respect, and their behavior and words are respectful of others, which in turn brings respect from others. They are honorable and will do the right thing. Real men cultivate relationships and recognize their need for others. They work to establish and maintain close relationships with their spouse, children, family, friends, and God.

It has been said that every man is limited by three things: The knowledge in his mind, the worth of his character, and the principles upon which he builds his life. It is our private philosophy of life and masculinity that determines our public performances as men.

All men would do well to memorize and heed this caution given by Jesus: "Woe to you men who think you have all the answers! You clean the outside of the cup and dish, but inside you are full of greed and self-indulgence. Blind men! First clean the inside of the cup and dish, and then the outside will also be clean" (see Matt. 23:25, 26, NIV).

CHAPTER 2

The Joy of Being Naked

Few things in life are as cute as a naked toddler running around with total freedom and abandon, unrestrained by cultural fences. As the presenter at a recent stress seminar I (Marvin) really got the group's attention when I remarked, "One of my most effective stress relievers is to look at a picture of a naked girl." Immediately I had their full attention! Reaching into my notebook, I then pulled out a picture of my granddaughter when she was 6 months old. She is lying on our bed and wearing nothing but a beautiful grin.

When I'm severely stressed, I pull out her picture and contemplate her freedom from stress and worry. It helps put things back in perspective for me. It also helps me remember what is really important in life, namely, my family and other close personal relationships, as well as taking time to enjoy life's simple pleasures.

Children love to run naked. They are not ashamed, and adults are not embarrassed when they see them. In fact, most adults usually react with delight as well. At what age do these childish delights become stifled by society's restraints?

When we moved to Hong Kong it was arranged for us to have dinner with a different family each night in order to make new friends. One night we were greeted at the door by a 2-year-old streaker running with wild abandon and glee. He is now in his late teens, and when we remind him of our initial introduction, society's restraints cause him to blush and feel embarrassed.

At what age do we lose the joy of being naked? Or do we?

At some age we begin to sense, or at least we are taught, that nakedness is shameful and that we must cover up that which is shameful. But what about the nakedness of our thoughts?

Most children are basically candid and inquisitive. My wife used to baby-sit other children, and I especially remember one little girl named Corky. She was a round-faced 5-year-old, and her name was appropriate. The first day I met Corky I was working in my upstairs study. I gradually became aware that somebody was watching me. Looking up from my work, I saw her little face peeking around the door and studying me carefully. "Well, good morning," I offered.

Without a direct reply she asked, "You know who you look like?"

"No," I said. "Who do I look like?"

Without hesitation she shot back, "Fat Albert!"

Well, that was Corky—brutally candid and to the point.

A child will often ask an adult about a scar, a withered hand, or a speech handicap. They ask in childish innocence, not with malicious forethought. At what age do we "learn" that being candid is not acceptable? Don't you find yourself as an adult male still wanting to know? Don't you sometimes still want to run naked—feel free—reclaim innocence?

Men learn to play a game called "the great cover-up." The rules are simple. Don't let anyone know what you are really feeling. Don't let others sense your true emotions. Really bold men might occasionally let others know what they think or how they feel about someone else, but they seldom reveal their inner selves. Men are taught not to risk being vulnerable.

In Colorado I recently attended a retreat for men in ministry. My reasons for attending were many: First of all, Colorado is a beautiful place. In addition, I was working on materials for a men's retreat, and I knew I could pick up valuable ideas. It was being presented by people I trusted. And I would be in a totally new, and

> **Men learn to play a game called "the great cover-up." The rules are simple. Don't let anyone know what you are really feeling. Don't let others sense your true emotions.**

presumably safe, environment. I was amazed at the depth of my personal needs that were revealed to me during this retreat.

We worshiped, prayed, and studied together in both large and small groups. We ate and walked and talked in informal combinations. We also listened to presentations by a variety of pastors and counselors who shared more than their knowledge—they shared themselves. They talked freely about their fears, frustrations, and temptations. Eventually we were asked to find a quiet corner and write about our inner thoughts and dreams. Then we gathered in groups of four with a Christian psychologist and were invited to share anything we felt comfortable in sharing. We spent a total of 10 hours in this more intimate environment, and the results were amazing.

I ventured to open a small window into my inner thoughts by sharing that my early life had involved a series of failed relationships. I did not have a strong relationship with my dad as a boy. I was frustrated and felt guilty about a continually failing relationship with God. Dozens of times I had responded to appeals to commit my life to God, but I never "felt" accepted by Him. My first marriage failed, and I saw it as primarily being my fault. I eventually told my group that things had greatly improved in recent years and that I now felt good about my relationship with my dad, my wife, and my God.

Our facilitator asked a few thoughtful questions about some of my feelings related to those earlier experiences. Soon I was sharing memories that I had not recalled since childhood and experiences that I had never shared with another human being.

I am well aware of the potential dangers involved in being open, honest, and vulnerable, but this experience changed my life. I became more emotionally naked with those four men than I have with anyone else in my life, and it felt good! I told them about the real me, and they loved me and embraced me anyway. For a few hours I experienced the joy of being naked without shame, disapproval, and embarrassment.

Men need someone they trust with whom to be naked. As much as men may enjoy being physically naked with their lovers, they also need someone with whom they can be emotionally naked. Men need someone with whom they can sit in the woods and share their frustrations, temptations, and failures. They need someone to unload with about work, finance, or family. It needs to be someone they can trust enough to share how angry they might feel with God at times and how guilty that anger makes them feel. Husbands may need to confide in their wives about how inept they sometimes feel as both a father and lover. Men need a safe environment in which they can strip "naked" and know that nobody will laugh or point fingers. They have a need to "bathe" and be "cleansed" emotionally and spiritually. Most males need the reassurance that other men have the same needs and fears that they themselves feel. Sometimes a man feels that he is the only one who has reason to be ashamed of his nakedness.

The good news is that Jesus Christ already knows you! He knows all about you, yet He died for you while you were still a hopeless sinner.

Some men go through life not wanting anyone to know their inner thoughts, but secretly wishing that someone would say, "I know *everything* about you, and I still love you!"

John Powell, in his book *Why Am I Afraid to Tell You Who I Am?* shares a statement made by a man he interviewed. "I am afraid to tell you who I am, because if I tell you who I am, you may not like who I am, and it's all that I have" (p. 12). We might paraphrase that to say: "I'm afraid to tell you who I am, because if I tell you who I am, you may not think that I'm a real man, and that image is all that I have."

The good news is that Jesus Christ already knows you! He knows all about you, yet He died for you while you were still a hopeless sinner. Jesus was tempted in all points like you, but He overcame those temptations. The good news continues with His promise to freely give that same power to you. The good news does not end with your relationship with Christ, but it actually fosters healthy relationships with others.

God created us as social beings, with a need for love and acceptance from other human beings. Husbands need to develop an emotional honesty and intimacy with their wives. Men also need to develop that same honesty with other men.

Intimate emotional relationships do not just happen. First, a man must recognize his need for them. Next, he must want them. Only then can he truly begin to cultivate intimate bonds.

"Dialogue is to love, what blood is to the body. When the flow of blood stops, the body dies. When dialogue stops, love dies and resentment and hate are born" (Reuel Howe).

A good way to begin is for you and your friend to read a book together. Select a book on marriage, relationships, midlife, or whatever appeals to both of you. If your friend is not too intimidated, you might read out loud to each other. Ask questions like How do you feel about that? or How would that work in your home? Keep the questions simple at first. Don't use this as an opportunity to unload right away. Just share and enjoy talking together.

You may wish to invite one or two others with whom you feel mutually comfortable to join you in a small study and prayer group. Make a commitment with each other that you will meet faithfully for perhaps three months. Let things flow easily, and don't force an agenda. Relationships take time to develop, but the rewards can be truly lifesaving.

This same approach can be used to establish a more intimate relationship with your wife. Browse through the contents of available books, and pick one that covers the topics you both would like to discuss together. It is so much easier to get into a personal subject when you have read together what someone else has to say about it. As you share your feelings about what this person has said, you will begin to convey messages about yourself in a less threatening manner.

How vital is honest communication between intimate human beings? In his book *The Miracle of Dialogue*, Reuel Howe reflects: "Dialogue is to love, what blood is to the body. When the flow of blood stops, the body dies. When dialogue stops, love dies and resentment and hate are born" (p. 3).

A word of sincere caution is appropriate here. While it is beneficial to develop and foster this intimacy with a male friend, it is not wise to choose another woman as a sharing partner unless she is your wife. No matter how noble your intentions, there is a bonding that develops with this level of openness. The history of well-intentioned Christian men is littered with casualties from caring relationships that got out of hand. Let's just say that if you don't play with fire, you stand a better chance of not getting burned. You certainly can have friends who are women, but if one is your best friend and confidant, she should also be your wife.

It is healthy that men are beginning to disrobe emotionally. Today they are beginning to think about their inner needs and struggles. Small groups are being formed that provide an atmosphere of safety and acceptance. Men have begun to talk about things like incest, alcoholism, spouse abuse, child abuse, and even homosexuality. But when the subject changes to lustful thoughts, mildly or explicitly pornographic material, sexual fantasies, or a host of other related topics, many Christian men begin to feel uncomfortable. Studies indicate that almost every man does struggle, to some extent, in one or more sexual areas, and he often feels guilty about it. Recognizing and admitting that even Christian men commonly have these struggles may be our first—and best—line of defense. Covering up, clothing ourselves with hypocrisy, will never cure our problems. We need to get "naked."

In a leading Christian journal a successful minister and conference speaker laid bare his struggles in the areas of lust and sexual temptation. Of course, he had to write anonymously. It is right that he did. He wrote about sharing his temptations with a trusted and respected friend. His friend, encouraged by this trust, then shared an even greater problem. As a result, these two men were able to lance their tortured consciences and allow the unhealthy guilt to drain away. Through acceptance, mutual strengthening, and nurturing, physical, emotional, and spiritual healing was able to take place. It should be noted that the counsel given in James 5:16 applies to women as well as men. "Therefore confess your sins to each other and pray for each other so that you may be healed. The prayer of a righteous man is powerful and effective" (NIV).

But where can one find a righteous man, since Scripture declares that "there is none righteous, no, not one" (Rom. 3:10; see also Ps. 14:3)?

A fundamental understanding of Christianity is that we are all counted as righteous through the merits of Jesus Christ. He imparts to us His mercy, love, and grace. When we become emotionally "naked" before Him, He calms our fears and covers us with His robe of righteousness. Adam and Eve attempted to cover their physical nakedness with fig leaves, but they were still emotionally and spiritually naked in God's presence. It is a joyful experience to strip everything away before Christ and know that He still accepts you. Likewise, you can model a similar experience of acceptance in a carefully chosen human relationship.

Although some think that it is normal for Christians to feel inadequate, it is abnormal after one has become "naked" before Christ. Yes, we are inadequate, but Jesus is more than adequate. We are unworthy, but He is worthy. "You are worthy, our Lord and God, to receive glory and honor and power, for you created all things, and by your will they were created and have their being" (Rev. 4:11,

God apparently loves the unique because He made each one of us so completely different.

NIV). "You are worthy to take the scroll and to open its seals, because you were slain, and with your blood you purchased men for God from every tribe and language and people and nation" (Rev. 5:9, NIV).

God apparently loves the unique because He made each one of us so completely different. Isn't that good news? As a result, we all see things from a slightly different perspective. Perhaps this story will illustrate the point.

After World War II a general and his young lieutenant were on a train in England. When they got on, the only seats left were across from a beautiful young lady and her grandmother. The two soldiers sat facing the two women. During their journey the train went through a long tunnel. For about 10 seconds there was total darkness. In the silence of the moment, those on the train heard two things—a kiss and a slap. Everyone on the train had his or her own perceptions as to what happened.

The young lady thought to herself, *I'm flattered that the lieutenant kissed me, but I'm terribly embarrassed that Grandmother hit him!*

The grandmother mused, *I'm aggravated that he kissed my granddaughter, but I'm proud she had the courage to retaliate!*

The general pondered, *My lieutenant showed a lot of guts in kissing that girl, but why did she slap me by mistake?*

The lieutenant was the only one on the train who really knew what happened. For you see, in that brief moment of darkness he had the opportunity both to kiss a pretty girl and to slap his general at the same time!

We all view incidents and circumstances through our own unique filters. God created you as a unique human being. Please accept your uniqueness as God's special love gift to you. Your nakedness is also God's creation. Your particular perception and perspective are valuable in the family of God.

Individually, we are like the group of blind men who were confronted with an elephant for the first time and tried to describe it. One felt the trunk and described the elephant as similar to a large snake. Another felt the tail and said that it was more like a rope. A third, feeling a leg, argued that an elephant was like a strong tree. Yet another, climbing a ladder and feeling an ear, was amazed at the others' descriptions, for he was certain an elephant was like a huge leaf. Each man was both right—and wrong.

Only as we put the picture together from many perspectives can we begin to get an accurate picture of anything, including ourselves. This is true in politics, in business, in the church, and in our own relationships. We need an open and honest dialogue with a close friend (or friends) to understand fully our *unique* love gift from God.

CHAPTER 3

Buddies, Partners, or Friends?

S ure I got buddies. I have allies. I have enemies. I have partners. And I have family. But I have no friends," confessed a
lonely man.

Isn't it ironic that buddies, partners, and friends are not synonyms
in male jargon? Many men today do not have a close male friend.
The sad fact is that most men simply do not trust each other enough
to become good friends. Men stare at, stalk, and survey each other,
but seldom reveal intimate details about their lives to other men.
From the start, from the initial handshake, the meeting of two men is
a face-off, a measuring against each other. Someone once compared
the introduction of two men to two dogs circling around and sniffing
each other.

Next time you're at a party, look around, and you'll often see
women grouped together on one side of the room, talking about their
feelings, family, and friends. On the other side, men will gather to
talk about sports, work, or politics. One of the reasons beer commercials are so popular on television is that they supposedly portray
male friendship. But what are men usually doing in these commercials? Watching sports. Hanging out. Arguing politics. Just getting
off from work.

While these are all relatively safe topics for male conversation,
and certainly can be stimulating, they do not develop the bonding
necessary for a true friendship. Men are actually hungry for real
friendship, but seldom allow themselves to be with another man just
because they enjoy each other's company. They must attend a sport-
ing event or congregate in the presence of many other males in order
to feel safe.

Male friendships follow predictable patterns of behavior based
on clues given to them at an early age.

1. Don't let your guard down (someone may "sucker-punch" you).
2. Don't show too much emotion (unless it's anger).
3. Don't become too involved, friendly, or frivolous.
4. Don't let on how much you really care.
5. Don't touch one another (except after scoring a basket or making a touchdown).
6. Don't act like a sissy or appear feminine in any way (adapted from author? *The Secrets Men Keep*, p. 97).

Many men view the need for a friend as a bit of an embarrassment, almost like they were immature and not totally self-sufficient.

Many men view the need for a friend as a bit of an embarrassment, almost like they were immature and not totally self-sufficient. Behind the bear hugs of camaraderie, men seem to be holding each other at arm's length. It's as if they need a buffer zone between themselves and other men. This space can be literally called a no-man's-land, where few men are willing to tread.

Men enter into friendships with other men, carrying with them the baggage of masculinity handed down to them by their parents and peers. I remember when my father told me that I was old enough to be a man. Although he never really spelled it all out, I understood that to mean no more crying or hugging. That's for sissies and wimps. A real man never shows his emotions and certainly does not come close to another man, lest someone think he might be gay. During my teen years there was even a prohibition (unwritten, of course) against wearing a pink shirt on Thursday, because only gays wore pink on that day.

When men delve into the unfamiliar territory of friendship, they find themselves ill-equipped to make real friends. Males are schooled in the areas of power, competition, one-upmanship, and winning at all costs. Men playing games aren't really playing. There must be a winner and a loser. Men are not taught how to share their feelings or to communicate them verbally to another man. Even though many men today have a clearer awareness of their need for emotional fulfillment, the pillars of maleness continue to be strength, invulnerability, and a competitive edge. Because of this male mystique, the only real friend many men have is their spouse. It is permissible to verbalize feelings to some extent with a woman, but never with another man.

In a survey of 1,000 people, Dr. Michael McGill, author of *Changing Him, Changing Her*, found that the change women want most is for men to talk about their feelings, and the change men want most is to be understood without having to talk about their feelings (Steven Naifeh and Gregory W. Smith, *Why Can't Men Open Up?* p. 4).

Some men feel confused by a woman's demand for honesty and openness, but they would be downright angered or threatened if another man made that same request. It's an unsettling time to be a man. All the old rules of male-female and male-male relationships are changing. Who can keep up with the current trend? Who even wants to? According to a number of surveys, the most important factor in a happy marriage or a bonding relationship is the ability by both parties to express their feelings to each other. One psychologist explained, "Men and women often speak different languages."

One woman made this comparison: "Our house was on a long, isolated stretch of beach. The water was so close you could hear the waves breaking against the rocks all day and all night. Wave after wave after wave. I used to think how we were like that, Tom and me. There I was, constantly washing up against Tom, but never getting anywhere. I was the wave, he was the rock. Does the rock talk to the wave? I suppose if I could have kept it up for centuries, I might have been able to wear him down a little" (Steven Naifeh and Gregory White Smith, *Why Can't Men Open Up?* p. 8).

When it comes to sharing emotions, men are often like a rock. Most men think that they are supposed to be competitive, aggressive, thick-skinned, and goal-oriented. A rock of strength and independence, unmoved by the flow of emotions around them. As Ernest Hemingway wrote, he is an "island in the stream." The river of life just seems to part and flow around him, and nothing short of a flood causes most men to take notice. That is not to say that all women are more sensitive than all men. Certainly there are men who openly display and express their emotions. However, men who are emotional are often shunned by the "rocks." Emotions are viewed as a feminine trait. Many men have almost a phobia against anything feminine in their personal lifestyle. Culture and peers have taught them that there is nothing worse than to be considered effeminate, which is often translated as being gay. This fear often prevents men from expressing feelings of love, concern, or compassion to another male, lest it be misunderstood. As a consequence, most men do not have an intimate male friend of the kind that they can fondly recall from boyhood or their teen years. Women, on the other hand, develop lifelong friends beginning in childhood.

Perhaps before the typical male can "reach out and touch someone" he must first learn how to reach inside and touch himself. A man often molds himself into something he is not. He feels what he *ought* to feel, wishes what he is *supposed* to wish, and likes what he *should* like. It is all a very neat package with no loose strings of emotions to get caught in the conveyer belt of life. Unfortunately, the package also precludes him from ever really experiencing the bond of intimate friendship with another male.

> *Perhaps before the typical male can "reach out and touch someone" he must first learn how to reach inside and touch himself.*

I (Len) recall fondly a bonding that occurred between me and a man almost 25 years my senior. I always thought that our relationship was like father and son, until one day we were talking and he said, "Len, I love you." Then tears welled up in his eyes. I choked up and almost inaudibly mumbled, "I love you too." As we hugged and slapped each other on the back (real men do not hug without pounding each other on the back) he concluded, "My only regret is that someone did not give me permission to say that 70 years ago."

How sad that men have been taught that it is not permissible to express verbally love to another man! As a man grows up and develops an adult personality, he builds up layers of control and repression. He is taught to deny his emotions or at least to express them in a way acceptable to the masculine role. Protecting his sense of manhood can become more important to him than developing close personal relationships. It is more important to be thought a man than to express how he really feels. Love for a woman often becomes sexual domination. Love for another man is a handshake or slap on the back. Love for a child becomes strong discipline or gift-giving. Sadly, many men walk through life in a suit of emotional armor lest anyone think them not manly.

The American male phobia about losing his "maleness" often precludes the kind of healthy close male camaraderie that exists in other cultures. Close male friends in many Mediterranean countries often show their friendship with lots of touching, slaps on the back, line dances, and warm hugs. Such behavior would be suspect in most American male gatherings. In America we allow back-slapping and butt-slapping only on playing fields, where it cannot be misunderstood as homosexuality. American male paranoia dictates that if we touch at all it must be brief and hard (like a punch or slap) and is best if it hurts just a little.

We seldom allow ourselves an opportunity to get to know other men in ways that permit a mutual exchange of feelings. As much as men do not seem to like to talk about their personal feelings, they love to talk about themselves and their accomplishments. Men seem to use the word "but" quite frequently, whereas women tend to use "and," from which we can infer that men are naturally more argumentative than women in our culture. "But" is the conversational crossed sword that sends two men into combat. Competition keeps men at a distance. Distance breeds ignorance. Ignorance breeds prejudice. And we are all the poorer because of it.

Opening our world to another man can eliminate many fears and insecurities. Through friendship with another man, we affirm ourselves as men and each other as human beings. We find that nothing is "wrong" with us, as we have secretly suspected in our self-imposed silence.

Two men met in a café along the waterfront, embraced robustly upon meeting (with the required slapping, of course), conversed briefly about some recent activities, then moved on to this dialogue:

"So, how are you really?"

"OK—as good as can be expected. You?"

"Same. I know what you mean."

"Yeah."

"Yeah . . ."

"Yeah . . . it's heavy . . ."

"It *is* heavy."

"It's not easy . . ."

"I know what you mean. It never is."

"But hey, no pain, no gain."

"Pain's good for you."

"That's what they say . . ."

"So, what else is new?"

Somewhere in that exchange, these two friends expressed financial pressure, physical ailment, marital trouble, and general fatigue and depression—maybe. Hopefully they both knew each other well enough to hear each other through the grunts and monosyllabic phrases. But what these two mostly expressed, even though they had difficulty putting it into words, was that they were not alone in their pain. Their pain was partly the result of male isolation and alienation, but these two men had crossed the precarious footbridge that connected their feelings.

Empathy is what male friends feel for one another. It lets men off the hook so that they don't have to verbalize their feelings in a way that might be embarrassing. Men tend to empathize their way through both communication and miscommunication, and never talk about it. However, can men really communicate and comprehend feelings without ever talking about them? I think not. There is too great a possibility for confusion, miscommunication, and misunderstanding. Realizing this, most men turn to women when they need to share their feelings.

Studies have shown that men with at least one close friend in whom they can confide have better psychological and physical health than men who do not.

Male friendships tend to lessen this almost codependent relationship men often have with women. Many men have been taught that only a woman can satisfy their emotional needs in relationships. Such teaching has virtually disqualified men as intimate companions. In fact, some men feel uncomfortable just thinking of the words "intimate" and "male" in the same sentence. One man lamented, "All my friends are women. I'm beginning to feel like one of the girls." This leaves men emotionally lopsided. Rather than demanding that women act like "one of the boys" or that men get in touch with their "feminine side," it would be more beneficial for men to develop intimate friendships with both males and females.

During those times when a man is having a crisis with a woman, there is really no substitute for an understanding, caring, and intimate male friend. Studies have shown that men with at least one close friend in whom they can confide have better psychological and physical health than men who do not. Loneliness is lessened by having a good support network that includes intimate friends with whom you can share feelings and frustrations.

Another benefit of male friends is the tendency to move from competition to cooperation with other men. Men who have developed close personal bonds with other men are able to support one another in a variety of activities. Personal and professional networking becomes more than a tool to advance your career.

Joanne Woodward, wife of Paul Newman, once commented on her husband's intimate relationship with Robert Redford. Their relationship developed during the filming of *Butch Cassidy and the Sundance Kid* and later *The Sting*. "When those two get together, forget about opening your mouth if you happen to be female. Bob and Paul really do have a chemistry. Someday, Paul and Bob will run off together. And I'll be left behind with Lola Redford" (quoted in *Why Can't Men Open Up?* p. 59).

History, literature, and the Bible all reveal the camaraderie and devotion between two men. Huckleberry Finn and Tom Sawyer, Tonto and the Lone Ranger, Butch Cassidy and the Sundance Kid, Captain Kirk and Mr. Spock, as well as David and Jonathan, are all examples of intimate relationships between two men. Such relationships are often deeper and more endearing than relationships between male and female. Perhaps it is because society and culture have taught men that where there are women, there is responsibility, but that where there are men, there is freedom.

Being with "one of the guys" allows a man to release built-up tensions and also reinforce his sense of sexual identity. Men often use

> **Men often use friendship with other men as a way of escaping the demands of the world, work, and family. It is a special, unpressured time when they can just "hang out" and not feel "hung out."**

friendships with other men as a way of escaping the demands of the world, work, and family. It is a special, unpressured time when they can just "hang out" and not feel "hung out." Unfortunately, most men have only golfing buddies rather than real friends.

Lyman Coleman relates a tragic story of male friendship. Tom tells the story: "I remember it was Friday and we were all going to take off work at noon so we could drive out, set up camp, and be ready to go first thing in the morning. I had one of those four-wheel-drive trucks, so the plan was that I would pick everyone up. Steve lived farthest out, so we always picked him up last. As it turned out, I didn't get away from work as early as I had hoped, and by the time I got Jim, we were running about an hour late. We pulled up in front of Steve's place and honked a couple of times. Usually he would have come running out, yelling about us being late, but this time there was no sight of him. I saw his gear back by the garage, and I thought maybe he didn't hear us. Jim stayed in the truck while I went around to get him. He was in the backyard, and he was dead. He had taken his shotgun, put the muzzle in his mouth, and with a piece of wood pushed the trigger and blown the back of his head away. He left a note near his body: 'I'm sorry. There is no one to talk to.'

"At first I was terribly angry. How could he do this? How could he say there was no one to talk to when there was me? I felt like I could have helped him, no matter what it was. We could have talked about anything. At least I thought we could. Only later did it hit me that I didn't really know if we could actually talk about anything or not, because we never really talked about much that was personal.

"I've spent a lot of time thinking about how much I was responsible for what Steve did because I wasn't the kind of friend he needed. I think I know now what Steve meant when he wrote, 'There is no one to talk to.'

"As close as I thought we were, I've come to see that we were never there for each other to talk to. Oh, we were there to do things with—hunt, fish, drink, play cards—but we were never there to talk about the things we were feeling, the things that might make you wonder whether or not life was worth living.

"I think now that what we called friendship wasn't really anything more than a casual and comfortable kind of acquaintance where we shared certain things at certain times, but we never shared ourselves. Maybe all relationships are like that. Lately, I've really tried to be more open with people, especially men. I've tried to build the kind of friendship Steve needed, because I believe I need that too. So far, it hasn't worked too well. Men get anxious when you talk about feelings, and it seems like the harder I try to get close, the faster the guys pull away. Maybe I am going too fast. But, for Pete's sake, if you go too slow you may never get there, or when you do it's too late, like it was for Steve" (Lyman Coleman, *Beginning a Men's Group*, p. 8).

Faithful friends are life's greatest treasure, and being a true friend has been one of the marks of being a real man. Thus, the betrayal of a true friend is painful and almost unforgivable. In Scripture, Judas betrayed his friend Jesus for 30 pieces of silver and a desire to gain power.

David wrote about the betrayal of a trusted friend with these bitter words: "Even my own familiar friend in whom I trusted, who ate my bread, has lifted up his heel against me" (Ps. 41:9, NKJV). In order to feel the agony of betrayal, one must have first experienced the joy of friendship and trust. Trust is the result of confidence, and confidence is developed through intimacy.

One Bible writer summed up friendship this way: "A friend [is one] who sticks closer than a brother" (Prov. 18:24, NIV).

The Bible relates a story of a great friendship between David (soon-to-be king of Israel) and Jonathan (son of the current king). If any two men ever had obstacles to friendship, these two men did. First, David had been anointed by the prophet Samuel as the next king of Israel when Jonathan should have been king by birthright. Furthermore, Jonathan's father, Saul, hated David and was determined to kill him. The risk to both men because of their friendship was high. David jeopardized his life by trusting Jonathan. When Jonathan argued David's case before his father, Saul threw a spear at him. Even with these obstacles, these men remained faithful to their friendship (1 Sam. 20).

Later, when David was faced with the sedition of Absalom, his son, and the defection of his trusted adviser and friend, Ahithophel, David prayed that God would confound the counsel of Ahithophel. God sent another friend, Hushai, to meet David's need during this time of crisis. It was the loyalty of a true friend that enabled David to regain the throne (2 Sam. 15:30-37). Ahithophel, on the other hand, tried to save his own life and eventually lost it (2 Sam. 16-17).

> *"A friend loves at all times" (Prov. 17:17, NIV). That means through the good times and bad. During times of stress and times of joy. During adolescence and midlife.*

True friends are more than acquaintances. "A friend loves at all times" (Prov. 17:17, NIV). That means through the good times and bad. During times of stress and times of joy. During adolescence and midlife. In fact, "Greater love has no one than this, than to lay down one's life for his friends" (John 15:13, NKJV). Notice how Jesus then affirmed His disciples by adding, "No longer do I call you servants . . . but I have called you friends" (verse 15, NKJV).

In order to learn how to be male friends, it is important to study the life and friendships of Jesus. True friends are dependable and can be counted on during a crisis. Crisis deepens true friendships but often destroys acquaintances and golfing buddies. Affliction is the strongest tester and formulator of friendships.

To prepare for male friendship, men should think consciously about developing themselves as friendly people. In addition to the story of David and Jonathan, read through the Gospels in the New Testament and notice how Jesus worked with people. Observe how He developed friendships through being trustworthy and dependable. Pattern His patience, nonjudgmental attitude, forgiveness, and acceptance in your own attempts to make true friends. Jesus was never severe or exacting except with self-righteous individuals who felt they didn't need anything or anyone in life.

What Is a Friend?

A simplified answer might be "A true friend rejoices with you in your success, and comforts you in your shame." A group of men at a male retreat made the following observations about friends:

• A friend is someone who knows all my faults and accepts me just as I am.

• A friend is someone who loves me enough to speak into my life and tell me the truth I need to hear.

• A friend is someone with whom I can be transparent, vulnerable, and honest.

• The measure of a friend is the degree to which I can share my life with him and not have it come back to me.

• A friend is someone I can count on in a crisis.

• A friend to me is like what Jonathan and David had in the Bible.

• A friend will not leave me or forsake me.

It is interesting how each definition of friendship actually describes Jesus. One of the great joys of being a Christian is developing an intimate friendship with Jesus.

Types of Friends

Best friends are our staunchest supporters. They will stick with us through the best and worst of times. They are the people whom we know intimately and with whom we can share our most private thought without fear that we will be rejected. This basic trust permits us to "bare our soul" without fear of reprisal. We can take off our "masks" and not feel self-conscious. Best friends express their anger when we have disappointed them, give affection when we have pleased them, and share openly about themselves and what really concerns them in life. Best friends are not afraid to take risks. Such friendships have withstood the tests of time and at least one major falling-out. This type of relationship is uncommon among men because it requires a large investment of time, attention, trust, conversation, self-disclosure, and the opposite of normal male competitiveness.

Good buddies are companions we can call on in time of need. Their friendships are important, too, but never involve sharing intimate details, fears, and insecurities of life. Good buddies are always available when needed, but never allow themselves to get too close. While they never have a discussion about their vulnerabilities or emotional struggles, they do have a great time going into battle together. Good buddies care more than they are ready to admit and often indirectly express their affection by being reliable. It is important for them to share tasks or goals, and they schedule time together to accomplish these. Good buddies get together to share a common interest, but they are reluctant to share their true feelings and will pull away from others who try to share with them.

Party friends are always available to have "fun" with. Depend on them to be ready to attend a ball game or racing event. Their talk is always superficial and deals with sports figures, statistics, and froth. Party friends like to share the good times, but are never around during the bad times. They are not someone you would be likely to call upon during a crisis. Because they are so superficial, they seldom spend more than a few hours with you before leaving for another "party."

Past friends may go all the way back to childhood. They share a common history or event. Possibly a next-door neighbor, school buddy, or

Best friends are our staunchest supporters. They will stick with us through the best and worst of times.

even best man. Past friends are a peg upon which we hang a bag of good memories and recollections. When getting together with past friends, you both slip into the old roles, tell the old stories, and recall the old times. It is a nostalgia trip, recalling time and memories shared and still treasured. Past friends are like living snapshot albums of our history and usually have little to do with our present lives.

Institutional friends are determined by our job or career. These friendships are maintained as long as our employment, church membership, or hobby interests remain the same. Most work associates and church friendships are on this level and are usually called acquaintances. Institutional friends relate to us on predictable levels and along predictable lines already established by the organization. Little is risked and little is gained other than a sense of belonging to a particular group. Conversation is usually limited to weather, work, economy, home repairs, lawn care, and other "safe" topics. Occasionally these friendships will deepen to party friends or even to good buddies, but seldom to best friends. It is likely that one or two institutional friends will become past friends when you change employment.

> **Jesus commanded: "Love each other as I have loved you" (John 15:12, NIV). Therefore, establishing friendship, trust, and love is not an option.**

How to Become a Friend

Friendship is part of God's plan for human beings. In fact, without friendship we are really subhuman, maybe even lower than wild animals, which establish some sort of relationship, often for life. Jesus commanded: "Love each other as I have loved you" (John 15:12, NIV). Therefore, establishing friendship, trust, and love is not an option. The question is With whom will I build this relationship? The following steps will help you become a friend.

1. Listen! Perhaps the single most important ingredient in any relationship is learning to listen actively, especially for the other person's feelings. By your attentiveness, by your expression of interest, and by keeping the conversation focused on him, not on you, encourage your friend to talk. While this is difficult for many males, it is not impossible. With practice, you can learn to listen so carefully that you "read" the other person's feelings and emotions.

2. *Enable!* Make it possible for the other person to fulfill his dreams and ambitions. While you may not play a direct role in his success or failure, you do play an important supportive role. Offer your friend encouragement, and pray for him daily. Be as specific in your prayers as your friend is specific in his dreams and ambitions.

3. *Affirm!* Let your friend know that you will be his friend through both the good and bad. Be reliable, dependable, and there when he needs you. When he is feeling lonely or depressed, be there! Let him know that you care and that he can depend on you.

As a frequent business flier, one man told of feeling sorry for himself when he boarded an airplane and found himself assigned to a middle seat. He hated middle seats. Then he spotted an old friend coming down the aisle who dropped down in the still-empty seat beside him for a chat. A few minutes later a voice over the intercom said, "If Mr. Harry Sommer is aboard, please identify yourself."

His friend raised his hand, and the flight attendant came to him and said, "Mr. Sommer, your ticket is in the first-class section today. Don't you want to come and take your seat in the forward cabin?"

Without hesitation his friend replied, "No, I'd rather stay here with my first-class friend."

The man in the middle seat smiled at the compliment,

Perhaps the single most important ingredient in any relationship is learning to listen actively, especially for the other person's feelings.

and several of the nearby passengers applauded. Shortly, however, the attendant returned. "Mr. Sommer, the main cabin is full today, but there is plenty of room in first class. Won't you come and take your seat, and bring your first-class friend?"

Friendship is giving up your seat in first class if it means interrupting your time together. Friendship is affirming the importance of your friendship in the presence of others.

4. Discern! Offer your friend perspective in his dreams, goals, ambitions, or failures. Help him see the broader picture than either success or failure paints on his canvas of life. What are the alternatives or other options that he might not see?

George Burns tells a story about having lunch with two dear friends—Jack Benny and Edgar Bergen. Jack Benny had a reputation for being tight. Burns often said that Benny had a "reach impediment" when it came to picking up the bill, and was, therefore, surprised to hear Benny ask for the check. On the way out Burns complimented Benny, "That was good of you to ask for the check."

"I didn't ask for the check," Benny protested, "and that's the last time I'll ever have lunch with a ventriloquist."

5. Commit! Make sure he understands that you are serious about a long-term relationship. If you are in your 20s, plan on knowing that person for the next five or six decades. Plan on living and sharing life together, growing old as friends. At each stage along the way, your friend will have changing needs. He will become, in a sense, a different person. You'll need to get reacquainted as your friend emerges from each stage of life. Your lifelong commitment to him will provide much-needed stability, which is often missing in our fast-paced, mobile society.

6. Pray! Think of specific areas in which your friend may be struggling. Take those issues to God in intercessory prayer. Ask God to work deeply in your friend's life and give both of you insight into the future and healing from the past.

7. Risk! Be vulnerable. Share your own fears and insecurities, encouraging your friend to do the same. As trust continues to develop between you, take even greater risks until there are no secrets between you.

It has been said that "friend-raising" is the secret to "fund-raising." Friends are life's greatest treasure. It is friendship that makes life worth living. It is friendship that provides strength during affliction. It is friendship that draws men closer to God. It is friendship that helps us understand God's plan of salvation. It is friendship that Jesus offers each person who comes to

Friends are life's greatest treasure.

Him with a trusting heart and a burdened soul. We know ourselves as we see ourselves in the eyes of a loving friend. Scripture reminds us, "Two are better than one, because they have a good return for their work: If one falls down, his friend can help him up. But pity the man who falls and has no one to help him up!" (Eccl. 4:9, 10, NIV).

Back in the late forties, just after the close of World War II, Jimmy Durante, the famous comic, got a call from Ed Sullivan. Ed wanted Durante to go with him to a veterans' hospital to entertain the wounded and disabled vets. Durante tried to beg off because he had a couple of radio shows to do. Sullivan promised that he could get back in time. Finally Durante agreed, but said he would be able to do only one short routine.

The two drove out the following Sunday, and Durante did his number. The audience was ecstatic and pleaded for more. What happened next surprised even Ed Sullivan, who was watching from the wings, well aware that Durante must leave immediately for the city if he was to make his radio date. Hearing the applause, Durante grabbed the mike and proceeded to do two more complete routines! When Durante finally left, to a standing ovation from the vets, Sullivan told him, "Jimmy, you were just great. But now you'll probably be late for your radio show—maybe even miss it."

Durante replied, "Look at that front row, and you'll see why I forgot all about those dates."

Ed Sullivan stuck his head through the curtain and spotted two soldiers in the center of the front row. Each had lost an arm, but they were applauding by clapping their two remaining hands together.

CHAPTER 4

Best-stressed Men
(Part 1)

Most Americans have learned a method of stress management from television commercials. The method is called 'pill popping.' The solution to nervous indigestion, tension headaches, alcohol-induced hangovers, sleepless nights, and a score of 'media maladies' is the magic bullet [tranquilizer] available at the drugstore. While some doctors are insisting that as much as 70 percent of all suffering derives from boredom, unhappiness, anxiety, and purposelessness, many continue to treat people as though their basic problem is a Valium deficiency" (Donald Ardell, *Fourteen Days to a Wellness Lifestyle*, p. 159).

Stress is a fact of life. If medication will not cure stress, what will? As a well-worn saying implies, how we deal with stress separates the men from the boys! I would like to suggest a 12-step approach that can make you a new man, if you *do* it! For easy recollection, the 12 steps fit neatly into the acronym C-R-E-D-I-T.

Choices

It is important to remember that you always have choices. A good practice in dealing with stress is to write down all your options. Open your mind to consider a multitude of possibilities—not just those that are obvious. The best solution for you may be neither obvious nor traditional.

I recently read of one man who really used his head. He was to make a presentation to a group of business executives the next morning in a town some distance away. He thought it might be less stressful if he drove there the evening before so that he could avoid the hassles of morning traffic. Upon arrival at his hotel he discovered that he had grabbed the wrong suitcase and that the only shoes he had were the jogging shoes he was wearing. Immediately he dashed off to the nearest mall, only to find no shoe store in sight and the mall closing in 10 minutes. What to do? Suddenly he had the answer. The next morning he limped into the meeting explaining that he had suffered an accident. (He had *accidentally* forgotten to pack his shoes!) His solution was neither obvious nor traditional, but it was creative and effective.

Recognizing that you are not the only one with problems and that other people's problems are often even more severe may help you put your own problems into perspective.

One choice is to look at other people's problems. Recognizing that you are not the only one with problems and that other people's problems are often even more severe may help you put your own problems into perspective. We all have problems. They won't go away by ignoring them, but choices help us realize that they could be worse.

You also might wish to consider some bad choices. These will make your other choices more appealing. It's kind of like the old saying, "Getting older is better than the alternative."

Take your time. Scrutinize, analyze, and prioritize your options. Share your list with a trusted friend or associate for additional input. Sharing often makes a stressful situation seem less threatening, especially when you examine all your options.

Relaxation

A physician notes what appears to be obvious—we live in an uptight world: "But the present world is a different one. Grief, calamity, and evil cause inner bitterness. . . . There is disobedience and rebellion. . . . Evil influences strike from early morning until late at night. . . . They injure the mind and reduce its intelligence and they also injure the muscles and the flesh" (cited in Herbert Bensen, M.D., *The Relaxation Response*, p. 15).

Interestingly enough, that was written more than 2,500 years before the birth of Jesus. Relaxation is a stress reducer! Not just fun activities, but deliberate relaxation that reduces stress. First, consider a full-length exercise. It is often referred to as a progressive muscle group relaxation technique. To do this you need to find a quiet comfortable setting where you will not be interrupted for at least 20 minutes. Seat yourself in a comfortable chair, place your feet flat on the floor, and rest your arms in your lap.

Begin with your facial muscles. Tense them by squinting your eyes tightly and holding for five seconds, and then relax those muscles. Repeat the same activity. Now open your mouth as wide as possible, stretching those facial muscles. Hold five seconds, relax, and repeat.

Now move down to the neck muscles. First, put your head forward with your chin on your chest. Hold, relax, and repeat. Now tilt your head back as far as you can. Hold, relax, and repeat. Continue the process with tilting your head toward your left shoulder and then your right. Each time hold, relax, and repeat.

Follow the procedure with each of the following actions. Keeping your feet on the floor, arch your back away from the chair. Then push against the back of the chair. Now tense up your buttocks. Next, tense up your thigh muscles, making them rigid. Work the lower leg muscles by first lifting your toes up as high as you can with your heels still on the floor. Then reverse the emphasis by lifting your heels with your toes still in contact. Now, curl your toes as tightly as possible without cramping.

Next, go back and do the arms by first making them rigid like someone was going to lift you by the elbows. Then clinch your fists and follow that by stretching your fingers out.

One final step is to do a total body awareness check. If you sense any tension or tightness in any of your muscle groups, go back and emphasize that area again.

A word of caution—don't overstretch. Stretching should feel good. Don't push it to the point of pain, which is counterproductive.

Now that you are totally relaxed, move on to the next step. Picture yourself in a familiar and very pleasant setting. It may be on a beach or on a mountainside or by a river. Put as much detail into your picture as possible. As you do this, close your eyes while you remain in your comfortable posture. Imagine the sky with its color. It may be clear or it may have some fluffy clouds. Picture the trees, flowers, and grass. Add sounds and even smells. If an unwanted thought or detail comes to mind, simply let it pass through. Don't get distracted. Once you are comfortable with your setting, try to imagine the warmth of the sun penetrating your body. Try to sense the waves of warmth and the sensation of heaviness in your arms resting in your lap and your feet against the floor. Continue the picture and the warmth for five minutes or so. (This is not self-hypnosis, but simply focusing your mind on a pleasant scene.)

Gradually end this exercise by refocusing on your surroundings. You may want to take a few deep breaths. You should feel extremely relaxed at this point. Don't be discouraged if you aren't completely successful the first time. Experiment with this process until it works for you.

Some may feel more comfortable and relaxed by contemplating some aspect of the life of Christ, such as His participation at the wedding feast or some other pleasant scene. Others find that they have a tendency to drift off to sleep during the last stage. That is not the desired result, although it is not altogether bad. You actually can reach a more relaxed level by remaining awake than if you nod off.

As a marathon runner, my resting pulse is quite low, usually around 48. During a thorough physical, my doctor confirmed that I (Marvin) had a very low heart rate, and he was pleased. "I can do better," I assured him. I then asked him to give me two minutes of quiet uninterrupted time just lying on the table. I focused on warmth and heaviness and in that two-minute period my pulse dropped to 36.

Deliberate relaxation will give your body a definite stress break. Give it a try.

Many men, when confronted with a stressor, are unable (for various reasons) to check out for a 20-minute relaxation break. What can you do for instant relaxation? Try the following.

1. When sitting at your desk, ask yourself, "Is it possible for me to lower my shoulders?" Most of the time you'll be amazed to discover that your shoulders can drop at least an inch. When we work we tense up

Take a walk. Even a minute out in the hallway away from the immediate sight of your stressor is helpful.

without realizing it. Get into the habit of asking yourself that question periodically throughout the day.

2. Take a deep breath. This is such a natural remedy. What do children most often do when they're frustrated? They give a sigh. A parent often responds, "Don't you sigh at me!" But actually the child is doing a stress-reduction exercise. Take a good deep breath, hold it for a moment, take in a little more air, and then slowly let it go. You can do this exercise in a group without detection. It feels good!

3. Take a walk. Even a minute out in the hallway away from the immediate sight of your stressor is helpful.

4. Keep a joke book handy, and read until something makes you chuckle. When you find something, share it with an associate so that you both can chuckle. This will be even more effective if it is an associate who sometimes gives you stress.

5. Take a good stretch. You might not be able to do a great one in some places, but you can do one or two muscle groups without creating a spectacle. The bottom line: *take time to relax.*

Exercise

"Until recently in human history, you had to be fit to survive. If you could not flee, fight, hunt, swim, and otherwise move about in short time spans under your own power, you would be left for the buzzards. Guess what? The forms have changed (there's a buzzard shortage), but the outcome is the same. If you are unfit, less opportunities and satisfactions will come your way, and more people will leave you behind. To be fit is to be able to play life's game with all the best equipment and preparation under optimal conditions. To be in poor shape is to handicap yourself unnecessarily, making life so much more difficult than necessary" (Ardell, p. 98).

Certainly you don't want to get *furniture disease*—that's when your chest drops into your drawers. Exercise not only prevents furniture disease, but it also is an excellent stress management tool. It is very difficult to handle stress effectively without an exercise program. Ironically, fewer than 20 percent of men have a regular exercise program. To qualify as a bona fide exercise program, it must meet certain criteria.

1. You need to exercise hard enough to do the heart some genuine benefit, but you do need to be careful here. This is especially true if you have not been exercising for some time. Most men tend to exercise the way they do everything else—fast and furious. You know, macho-like. Put a man on a jogging trail and let a fit, well-trained woman pass him by, and he will nearly kill himself trying to keep up. Eventually he branches off on another trail, where he will spend the next 10 minutes trying to regain both his breath and his composure.

Take it easy. You should be able to carry on a conversation throughout your exercise program. Even world-class athletes do this. For a champion marathoner a conversational pace might be a 5½-minute mile. For the average man it might be a 10-minute mile. It doesn't

> **You don't want to get furniture disease—that's when your chest drops into your drawers, so exercise is not an option. Exercise not only prevents furniture disease, but it also is an excellent stress management tool.**

matter. In the words of a famous shoe manufacturer, "*Just do it!*"

2. Sustain the exercise for at least 30 minutes. Once you determine the effort level required to reach the target heart rate, keep it going for the 30-minute period. Your body switches from burning carbohydrates to burning fat after about 20 minutes. Your heart muscle also needs this sustained exercise for maximum health.

3. Repeat the effort at least four times per week. Five times would be even better. One of the most dangerous patterns of exercise is weekend athletics. A man who works hard all week, endures all manner of stress, and then plays hard on the weekend is a heart attack waiting for a place to happen—especially if he is older than 35.

Make an exercise program part of your regular routine. You have the time. You just don't take it. Everyone is given 24 hours each day, and each man determines how he will spend them.

4. Make it enjoyable. Do something you really like to do. Few people are going to stick with an exercise program if they hate every minute of it. Vary the routine. Jog one day, swim one day, bike one day, walk one day, and play racquetball one day. Do some exercises with friends and some alone. Do some indoors and some outdoors. Your choices are many, after you make the first choice—to exercise. You will also find that you feel less tired and sluggish if you exercise when you get home from work rather than plopping down in front of the television.

For those of you who must do multiple things together, go for a walk with your wife and/or your kids. At a conversational pace you can enjoy family time and exercise at the same time. Exercise has improved my life in many ways. Within six months after beginning a running program (I actually love running) in 1979, I lost 55 pounds, dropped my blood pressure 20 points, and lowered my resting heart rate 24 beats per minute. You will have similar results, depending on how out of shape you are now and how faithfully you exercise.

A word of caution: If you have not been exercising according to this criteria, check with your personal physician before you begin. This is especially important if you are over 35, overweight, a smoker, or your family has any history of heart trouble. It is good advice for every man to have a physical exam before beginning a serious exercise program.

Diet

Dr. Donald Ardell describes six types of eaters:

1. Survivors—who eat simply because they must, but with little or no interest.

2. Vaudevillers—who view food as entertainment. Emphasis is on taste and the other senses.

3. Disease avoiders—who are obsessed with "scare" research. Their goal is to avoid carcinogens.

4. Fat fighters—an unhappy lot who tend to eat like vaudevillers, but live in guilt and diet worlds.

5. Food faddists—who shop mostly in "health-food stores" and blend wheat germ, Valium, and bonemeal every morning. Ardell mentions one friend who is so iron rich she attaches her earrings with magnets.

6. Health enhancers—who eat for health, enjoyment, and performance. Ah! May their tribe increase.

The key is simplicity and common sense. There are some regular offenders in most males' daily routines that have accumulative results. Caffeine, fat, refined foods, and sugars can all be bad for you, as well as tobacco, alcohol, and drugs of choice.

Everyone eats some fat, some refined foods, and some sugar, and most men will use some forms of drugs on occasion. What you should be concerned about is the accumulative effect upon your body. Again, it is a matter of awareness and evaluation.

What is a day like in the life of a not-too-untypical man? It often begins with a rude and noisy alarm clock. Imagine that! We have programmed ourselves to begin with a clanging bell or buzzer that literally jolts us into the day. Nice soft music would be much better. Most men begin the day with stress!

Whenever you are confronted with a stressor, imagined or real, your blood vessels constrict and focus their feeding more on the internal organs. Adrenaline is sent into the blood, which increases the heart rate. As the result of increased heart rate and constricted vessels, the blood pressure rises. At the same time, coagulants are pumped into the blood stream as a precaution in case of bleeding. All because of a noisy alarm clock? You bet. The body cannot differentiate between the stress of a screaming child and the stress of a jangling alarm.

We have programmed ourselves to begin with a clanging bell or buzzer that literally jolts us into the day. Nice soft music would be much better.

Stumbling from his bed, the typical man heads toward the kitchen for a cup of coffee to clear the cobwebs. But caffeine constricts his blood vessels and increases his heart rate even more. Adrenaline and caffeine are related drugs.

If the typical man smokes a cigarette with his cup of coffee, he'll get more blood vessel constriction, more stimulation to the heart, and even higher blood pressure because of nicotine, another relative of the adrenaline-caffeine family.

Before leaving for work, the typical male might eat a jelly doughnut with his second cup of coffee. Ah, real food! Having filled his special travel cup with more coffee, he jumps into the car and heads for work. Rats, wouldn't you know it, another traffic jam! More stress. He's going to be late again. He's going to miss his first appointment. "Hey, buddy, don't try to cut in front of me!" Finally, he arrives at work with seconds to spare. "Now let's see, where are those papers? Oh no, I left them on my desk at home!"

Midmorning brings a welcome respite for another coffee break and a sweet roll. The rest of the morning brings its routine portion of problems as well. Finally it's time for lunch—a luncheon appointment. Since he hasn't eaten much today, something a little rich sounds good, followed by a nice dessert. Of course, he's not aware of the fat deposits slowly accumulating on the inside of his arteries.

After lunch the day continues with more deadlines, some good news, and some bad news. His body reacts to both the positive and the negative stress. At last the day is over. More traffic on the way home. He arrives home wound up tight and tries to unwind with an alcoholic drink. The stress of the day is now compounded by the fact that his drink measurably thickens the blood. Soon it's time to enjoy another heavy meal (probably eaten in front of the television), and finally he collapses into bed after watching the late news, most of which was also very stressful.

As you can see, it is not just one deviation from the ideal in a day's time, but rather the piling on of multiple factors. Nobody is going to avoid them all, believe me. But you can avoid a significant amount and change your stress level.

Let me suggest a more healthy typical day. Use a clock radio to start the day with music. If you are in the habit of a hot drink early in the day, find an herbal tea or coffee substitute that you enjoy. Eat a balanced breakfast. It doesn't have to be a big meal, just balanced. Include some grains and fruit. Leave early enough to allow for possible traffic delays. If you get to work a little early, take some time to read something for yourself, write a letter, or take a short walk before you begin.

Use some relaxation techniques during the day. With just a little more thought, pick your lunch foods. There are lots of good options. And don't always schedule business with lunch. Take a real break from stress.

When you get back home take a walk, enjoy an activity time with your family or friends, and then enjoy a light meal. Supper can be filling without being hard to digest. If you're married, spend some time with your family in a mutually enjoyable activity (which might include a television program) that is varied from night to night. Schedule some talk time with your wife before you retire. Finally, go to bed early enough to feel truly rested the next morning.

Individuality

Have you noticed that men and women are different? Ever since I made that discovery I've been rather fond of most of the differences and have never been able to understand why some people want to make us alike.

Looking past the obvious, you will soon discover that we are all different. In fact, the laws of genetics predict that the chances of two people being identical are about one in 280 billion. You are truly one of a kind!

How do you feel about being you? Have you ever secretly wished that you were someone else? Have you ever wished that you could be more like someone else? Most of us have cherished those fantasies at some time in our lives. But if we look at each other more objectively, we'll have a lot less stress.

I love my uncle Vernon. I've always considered him my favorite because he's such a unique individual. In other words, most people think he's nuts! He did spend a number of years as the personal guest of the governor of the state of Washington. Let's just say that he "stole" the opportunity. One event that impressed me occurred at my grandma's house. Uncle Vernon walked in right at dinnertime, and of course, Grandma asked him if he would like something to eat.

"No," he replied, "I'm not that hungry. I'll just have a light lunch." With that he reached up, unscrewed the lightbulb, smashed it in his hand, and swallowed the glass. I was impressed. It certainly was low-fat, low-calorie, low-sugar —and it had fantastic fiber!

How do you feel about being you? Have you ever secretly wished that you were someone else?

If you could meet the rest of my family, you'd discover that most are unique characters. I love their individuality. Isn't it too bad that in many Christian churches we spend so much time trying to clone people? How many fathers have been disappointed when their sons didn't follow in their occupational or athletic foot-steps?

Reduce your stress by accepting your individuality. Serenely accept it as it is. Then, also allow your spouse, your children, your boss, your colleague, and everyone else you come in contact with to be unique.

Time

Time is another one of those constant pressure sources. There never seems to be enough of it. Sometimes I wonder why God didn't make longer days. Actually, we all have the same amount of time each day, but some people appear to have a lot more fun than others. Why? The answer is simple—priorities! Here are a few very simple suggestions that have helped me manage my time and set priorities.

1. Make a list. I do this every day. Before I finish a day I look at my list and transfer anything that isn't checked off onto a new list for tomorrow. Then I add any new items that I need to accomplish. It doesn't have to be a crisis item to get on my list. It might only be something that I need to remember to do.

2. Prioritize. Go down your list and circle in red any items that absolutely must be finished that day. By checking back with your list during the day, you will be reminded, less stressed, and most likely to get it done. Other items may not have to be completed until a later date, or you may work on only part of them. If you have something coming up in a week or two that you're simply afraid you might forget, put it on your list. Then keep transferring each item to your next day's list until it becomes a higher priority. You might even do that for your wife's birthday and other important dates.

Richard Foster in *The Freedom of Simplicity* suggests prioritizing in this manner: List all activities for one month and then rank them:

a. absolutely essential
b. important, but not essential
c. helpful, but not necessary
d. trivial

Then eliminate all the threes and fours as well as 20 percent of the ones and twos. He concludes: "We are too busy only because we want to be too busy. We could cut out a great deal of our activity and not seriously affect our productivity" (p. 92).

3. *Value your time.* We all waste time. I'm not even sure that we should try to overcome all of that.

Most of us probably waste too much time. Try to reclaim some of it.

But most of us probably waste too much time. Try to reclaim some of it. Listen to books on tape as you drive. Take a book with you to read when you have to wait. Consider time as money, and save it whenever possible.

Try reclaiming some of your evening time. The average man spends three hours a day watching TV. Do you realize that works out each year to six and a half weeks of 24-hour days glued to a chair? Even if you watch only one hour a day, it amounts to two weeks. I'm not suggesting that you should throw out the TV. I like sports too. I am urging that you evaluate and value your time. There is more of it available than you think. Most of us just don't use it wisely.

CHAPTER 5

Best-stressed Men (Part 2)

O nce your first C-R-E-D-I-T check has been approved and become a part of your daily life, you are ready for more
CREDIT. Remember, don't make your C-R-E-D-I-T check
another source of stress. This acronym is meant to alleviate stress,
not create more of it.

Communication

Lack of communication is often the primary cause in failed relationships. This is true in marriage, parenting, or business. Men,
by nature and influenced by culture, are usually not very good
communicators. Men are good at giving lectures or instructions,
but they are seldom good listeners or comfortable with sharing
their feelings. Somehow men have learned that it is not masculine
to express emotion, tenderness, or feelings other than various
forms of anger.

Isn't it amazing that before marriage most men are quite romantic?
They buy flowers and whisper sweet phrases. Unfortunately, once a
man has "caught" his prize, he tends to revert to more traditional male
behavior, which denies feelings and makes him a poor communicator.

It's like the wife who complained to her husband, "You never say
you love me!"

"What do you mean?" he responded angrily. "Don't you remember the night I asked you to marry me? Don't you recall how I looked
into your eyes and told you how much I loved you?"

"Of course I do," she sighed. "I'll never forget that night, but
that was 28 years ago."

"Well," he countered defensively, "if I ever change my mind, I'll
let you know."

To have less stress in your life, deliberately seek out opportunities to say loving or affirming things to those you care about. If

you're a father, tell your children that you love them. It may be hard for you at first, but you'll never be sorry that you did. Soon they'll be grown, and it may be too late.

Sometimes what we don't do is just as important as what we do.

Take the time to express your love to those you truly care about. Frequently tell those whom you care about that you love them both for the things they do and those they do not do. The best way to solve a problem is to have affirmed that person on a regular basis prior to the problem. Affirmation builds trust. Trust holds a relationship together while problems are being worked out.

> **Take some time out just to play or to enjoy a relaxing hobby. Save yourself a future doctor bill by taking time to recreate yourself today.**

If you have a disagreement with a family member or a colleague, exercise common sense and tact, but get the problem out on the table where you can deal with it. If you absolutely cannot find the courage to bring up the problem verbally, then write a letter. Express how you feel, good or bad, and ask that person for an opportunity to talk it through.

Rest

There are at least three aspects of rest. The first one is sleep. The average individual needs seven to eight hours of sleep per night. Occasionally, some can get by with less for a while, but it is not recommended as a lifestyle. Recent studies are shedding new light on this subject, but most men still need to get adequate rest. If you have any concern about your lack of rest, sleep on it.

In *The Complete Book of Running* the late Jim Fixx wrote about the benefits of proper rest. His advice is valid whether you're running in a marathon or running under emotional stress. "Runners need plenty of sleep. Fatigue tends to accumulate quickly if you don't sleep enough, leaving you listless, unenthusiastic, and susceptible to colds. Sometimes job and family responsibilities, late-night television, and a daily running regimen make it hard to find time for enough sleep. If you can bring yourself to do it, turning the set off a half hour earlier works wonders" (p. 180).

The second part of rest is recreation. Take some time out just to play or to enjoy a relaxing hobby. Save yourself a future doctor bill by taking time to recreate yourself today.

When I was in college I was preparing for my senior year comprehensive exams, and I was really pushing the limits. The final weekend I stayed up late Saturday night and began again Sunday morning after about four hours of sleep. I had so much memorization to do that I needed to cram all day Sunday. Finally, about midafternoon, I could study no more. I took a bat, a ball, my two sons with their gloves, and headed out the door.

"Where are you going?" queried my wife. "Are you sure you have time for that?"

"If I don't take time for this, I'll never make it through the next 24 hours anyway," I responded as we headed out the door. We played hard for about two hours. I came back and studied for a few more hours, went to bed at a decent hour, and aced the exams on Monday. I just needed to play for a while. There is no substitute for hard work, to be sure, but neither is there any substitute for balance and recreation.

Develop some hobbies. Read some good books. Volunteer. Join a new group. Enroll in a class. Play with your kids. Play with your wife. Take time to build some fun into your routine. Try it, you'll like it!

The third piece of this rest trilogy is the Sabbath. The word "sabbath" literally means rest. Spend this day with God, and don't allow any of the pressures of this earth to come between you and Him. Focus on His love, His goodness, His Word, His mercy and grace, His creation, His plan, or any other of the endless attributes of God.

"Six days do your work, but on the seventh day do not work, so that your ox and your donkey may rest and the slave born in your household, and the alien as well, may be refreshed" (Ex. 23:12, NIV).

Both authors love the weekly Sabbath day. By the time the sun goes down they are eagerly anticipating their special day with God. The bills, deadlines, and problems (for the most part) are still going to be there the next day, but for 24 precious hours we choose to put them aside and walk with Jesus. What a privilege! Whatever your denominational persuasion, you need the rest promised on the Sabbath day.

Evaluation

This is another vitally important aspect of stress management. First, begin your evaluation by keeping a stress diary for one week. Write down each time that you feel stressed. Note the time of day, the cause (the stressor), how it made you feel (describe the actual physical symptoms), what you did about it, and whether your actions increased or decreased your stress.

At the end of the week, review your diary. What patterns have developed? Does most of your stress come in the morning, afternoon, or evening? Is more of it job-related or family-related? Is it external (things that happen to you) or internal (things that you worry about)? Is it caused by things that you can do something about or by things that are beyond your control?

Once you have discerned a pattern, honestly evaluate what you can do about it. A better breakfast might eliminate morning stress. An exercise program might relieve evening stress. A relaxation exercise might help with internal stress. Improving communication skills might alleviate external stressors. You'll find your stress diary both challenging and revealing.

Second, evaluate your body. I mean take a long, hard, honest look! The best way to do this is in front of a full-length mirror—and be sure to wear the same outfit you were born with. What do you see? Do you like it? Be honest, but also be fair and balanced. If you're over 40, you're never going to look like 20 again. On the other hand, if your profile looks like your mother the day before you were born, you need to admit that you have furniture disease and find the courage to rearrange your furniture! In this case, your lifestyle.

Your body is a wonderful thing. Thank God for it. Appreciate it and love it even if you will never qualify for a calendar modeling session. "For you created my inmost being; you knit me together in my mother's womb. I praise you because I am fearfully and wonderfully made; your works are wonderful, I know that full well" (Ps. 139:13, 14, NIV).

Self-appreciation and self-love involve giving yourself the time and opportunity to enjoy optimal health. Take another look in the mirror as you write out some realistic goals for change. Then commit yourself to those changes.

Finally, evaluate your relationship with God. Do you make time for God on a daily basis? Do you allow Him to lift your burdens? How much of your life is purposefully available for God to use? Claim these promises as God's gift to you. "Do not let your hearts be troubled. Trust in God, trust also in me" (John 14:1, NIV). "Come to me, all you who are weary and burdened, and I will give you rest. Take my yoke upon you and learn from me, for I am gentle and humble in heart, and you will find rest for your souls. For my yoke is easy and my burden is light" (Matt. 11:28-30, NIV).

God is willing to accept you just the way you are. Not one single change is required for total acceptance. But someone once noted, "God loves me just the way I am, but He loves me too much to let me stay that way."

Self-appreciation and self-love involve giving yourself the time and opportunity to enjoy optimal health.

It would be helpful to spend an hour each day reflecting upon scenes from Christ's life, especially the scene of Calvary. One super meditative exercise is to read—better yet, memorize—some of your favorite hymns. This is one of my personal favorites that I find especially meaningful when under stress.

Cover With His Life
"Look upon Jesus, sinless is He;
Father, impute His life unto me.
My life of scarlet, my sin and woe,
Cover with His life, whiter than snow."

Do It

Even simple lifestyle changes are of no benefit unless you do them. Pick at least one area you want to improve upon—and begin! The time to begin a stress-reducing lifestyle is now—not tomorrow.

"I AM"—The Lesser One

Do you ever feel like you are trying to run in competition with the great "I Am"?

"Moses said to God, 'Suppose I go to the Israelites and say to them, "The God of your fathers has sent me to you," and they ask me, "What is his name?" Then what shall I tell them?' God said to Moses, 'I Am who I Am. This is what you are to say to the Israelites: "I Am has sent me to you"'" (Ex. 3:13, 14, NIV).

Men sometimes feel like they are supposed to be all-knowing and all-powerful. Men often try to be God or at least His right-hand man. As a man I have often felt that I am supposed to be a handyman, plumber, mechanic, landscaper, etc. The problem is, I don't enjoy those things at all. My coauthor, Len, does. However, I do have other interests and skills. For example, my wife appreciates the fact that I take time for her. I even enjoy going shopping with her. I help with household chores. Besides all that, I helped raise a son who is a good handyman and mechanic. I can rightfully get partial credit for that.

Since you are not omnicompetent, remember that human and divine help is only a request away. When you have problems that are weighing heavily upon you or relationships that are showing signs of stress, you can reach out for help. When life really begins to close in on you, one of the most effective ways of gaining a proper perspective is to help someone else. In the vast majority of cases you'll find that your problems seem a bit more manageable after helping someone else.

> **When life really begins to close in on you, one of the most effective ways of gaining a proper perspective is to help someone else.**

The bottom line is to remember that while your problems and stressors are real and you should not ignore them, in the scope of eternity they are not quite as significant as they first appear.

Trust

I have a thought process I have used since I became a Christian that really works. When I'm faced with a real stressor, I ask: How bad can it be? Then I remind myself: I can be fired. I can be robbed. I can be beaten. I might lose my family, my health, my wealth, even my life. But no one can take away my relationship with Jesus Christ.

"If God is for us, who can be against us? . . . Who shall separate us from the love of Christ? Shall trouble or hardship or persecution or famine or nakedness or danger or sword? . . . No, in all these things we are more than conquerors through him who loved us. For I am convinced that neither death nor life, neither angels nor demons, neither the present nor the future, nor any powers, neither height nor depth, nor anything else in all creation, will be able to separate us from the love of God that is in Christ Jesus our Lord" (Rom. 8:31-39, NIV).

As much as a man may love his family, his relationship with Christ is by far the most secure relationship that he can possess. No matter how bad things get, Jesus is Lord, and He has the situation well in hand.

CHAPTER 6

The Male Obsession!

The male preoccupation with sex in general and his genitals in particular often borders upon obsession. Studies indicate that the average male between the ages of 12 and 20 thinks of sex approximately 20 times per hour (Warren Farrell, *Why Men Are the Way They Are*, p. 121). Isn't it amazing that male teenagers can survive seven years of sexual thoughts every three minutes?

Although the male role has been challenged and changing during the past two decades, one area of masculinity has changed little throughout recorded history, namely, the male obsession with sex. For centuries men have been conditioned to view themselves through the phallic lens of masculinity. Jack Litewka referred to it as the process of "socializing the penis"—a process that has distorted male behavior, emphasized the penis as the center of man's identity, and caused men to view women as objects to be dominated and conquered.

Men today are confused about what it means to be a "real" man. The term has become almost a cliché. They find it difficult to give up the old manners, the old rules, the old games that they were taught to play as men. It is hard to get rid of the notion that the male function is to be a warrior and worker in all areas of life, especially sex. This mistaken concept often creates tremendous stress in relationships in which the male is viewed as a *sex machine*, always ready to function at a moment's notice. The inability to function upon command makes most men feel like a failure as a male.

Because of his social and cultural conditioning, the average man thinks of himself as an initiator, dominator, and controller. Therefore, it is especially difficult for the modern man willingly to give up power that he has received as a birthright through centuries of male domination. Men have taken such power for granted, and many feel threatened when it is challenged. Loss of power, or even the threat of loss, can drastically affect male sexual behavior. Everything from impotency to date rape can find its roots in low self-esteem in males. Frustration and fear cause some men to retreat and regroup, whereas it prompts others to lash out violently in a futile attempt to reclaim lost power.

According to the media, men have changed right alongside women. Television and movie scripts showcase househusbands and male consciousness-raising groups. Thousands are reported as joining the ranks of liberated males. Technically, these numbers are correct. Unfortunately, a few thousand liberated males have not made a significant impact on the other 100-plus million who are resistant to change.

The story is told of a young man buying a shirt in a department store. The shirt label read "shrink-resistant." Curious, the young man inquired, "What does shrink-resistant mean?"

"Oh," replied the clerk, "it means that the shirt will shrink, but it doesn't want to."

The average modern male wears a "change-resistant" label. He'll change, but he really doesn't want to. The truth is that the concept of masculinity has not changed significantly during the past 20 years. Few men have had their consciousness raised, and househusbands are still scarce. The majority of American men are uncertain, confused, and downright angry about who they are and where they are going.

Men are changing much more slowly and reluctantly than women. For the first time in recorded history, men must adapt to a loss of power in the war between the sexes. It's a new experience for them, and many men don't like it. When it comes to change, women are the active agents today, not men. To implement change, men must first divest themselves of real or perceived power and status, and change encounters its greatest resistance in the last male stronghold—sex!

The majority of American men are uncertain, confused, and downright angry about who they are and where they are going.

Whether men admit it or not, they are actually dependent upon women to define their masculinity. The common denominator for almost every male is his desire to achieve acceptance by a female. Most men have been culturally conditioned to have close bonds only with their sexual lovers. In most cases, their lovers are female.

The rules have changed, and women are no longer dependent upon men to affirm their sexuality or provide security. As the female has become more self-sufficient, the male has become even more dependent upon her to affirm his masculinity. This unhealthy dependency has resulted in an increased emphasis upon male sexual dysfunction.

> *As the female has become more self-sufficient, the male has become even more dependent upon her to affirm his masculinity. This unhealthy dependency has resulted in an increased emphasis upon male sexual dysfunction.*

Traditional Christian cultures are often suspicious of pleasure, negative toward sex, and tend to overreact if sex and pleasure are mentioned in the same paragraph. Many Christians believe that the human body is fundamentally a sinful object and that sexual energy is dangerous unless channeled in carefully prescribed ways. Children are often taught that their genitals are dirty and shameful. Conditioned by the Victorian era, many Christian males still view sexuality as shameful. As a consequence, some Christian men have become grossly distorted sexual caricatures, bearing little resemblance to the original Adam.

Correcting Victorian distortions about male sexuality will require change! This may not be easy, since some men fear change almost as much as they fear women, although few men would willingly admit to either condition. The change I am proposing is not some bold, new flight of fantasy into the future, but a biblical look back into the past.

"The Lord God formed the man from the dust of the ground and breathed into his nostrils the breath of life, and the man became a living being. . . . The Lord God took the man and put him in the Garden of Eden to work it and take care of it. . . . The Lord God said, 'It is not good for the man to be alone. I will make a helper suitable for him.' . . . So the Lord God caused the man to fall into a deep sleep; and while he was sleeping, he took one of the man's ribs and closed up the place with flesh. Then the Lord God made a woman from the rib he had taken out of the man, and he brought her to the man. . . . The man and his wife were both naked, and they felt no shame" (Gen. 2:7-25, NIV).

Adam and Eve were both created as sexual beings. It was the Creator's design and choice to make humans sexual. There was no shame associated with their sexuality. Shame did not enter into the human psyche until sin began to determine human behavior. Shame was created by sin, not by God. Sex was created by God, not by sin. It is sad that many Christians still view sin, shame, and sexuality as synonymous. As a result, for many Christians sin still distorts their view of masculinity, causing myths to be accepted as facts.

Myths of Masculinity

Myth of the penis—Men often relate to their penis as a priceless piece of plumbing that defines their identity as a male. Sometimes men feel victimized by their capricious organ that seems to have a mind of its own. So important is the penis that if it does not respond upon command, men either view themselves as less than a man or blame their spouse in order to preserve their male identity. This myth is obviously a distortion, since it makes male identity revolve around the penis in a way that female identity does *not* revolve around the vagina.

Throughout history exaggerated, erect phallic symbols have been placed on temples, military standards, and art objects. Only the Greeks were content to portray the penis in passive repose. Both ancient and modern cultures often promote the erect penis as evidence of exuberant masculinity. While I (Len) was stationed in Japan, shortly after the Korean War, I witnessed a religious procession in which a 40-foot log, carved to resemble an erect penis, was carried through the streets to celebrate the gift of fertility. Pagan religions often venerated the erect penis as a symbol of fertility and even resurrection power.

"Phallic resurrection has to do with the capacity of the male member to return to life, time and again, after defeat and death. Each time the phallus explodes in orgasm, it dies. Energy pours forth from the phallus as the fountain of life in great excitement, and its time is over. A man is spent. Quiet returns, a desire for rest falls upon a man as though he were falling into the grave—his need for sleep" (Keith Thompson, ed., *To Be a Man*, p. 129).

Myth of male hormones—Both men and women use this myth to justify aggressive male behavior and perpetuate the lie that men are incapable of expressing their feelings. Men are seen as aggressive, sexual, nonfeeling animals who have little choice in their actions because of male hormones.

According to Dr. John Money: "There really is no such thing as a 'male hormone' in the sense that men have certain hormones that cause them to behave in a certain way. There are three hormones (estrogen, testosterone, and progesterone), and both men and women have all three of them. So there are really only 'people hormones'" (Steven Naifeh and Gregory White Smith, *Why Can't Men Open Up?* p. 34).

The difference in male/female behavior is the *threshold* at which behavior is triggered, not in the behavior itself. Both men and women have the capacity for aggressive, sexual, or nonfeeling behavior.

In one study a baby monkey was presented to an adult female monkey. It took only a split second for the adult female monkey to begin parenting the little fellow. Almost immediately she cuddled the baby and snarled at anyone who approached the young one. Later the same baby monkey was placed with an adult male monkey. Initially the adult male just sat there, seemingly indifferent to the baby monkey as it pestered him for attention. After five minutes of persistent pestering, the message finally got through to the male monkey's brain, and he then began to cuddle and protect the baby just as the adult female monkey had. Yes, both males and females have the potential for the same intimacy patterns and behavior. However, the thresholds at which intimate behavior is triggered differ according to one's hormonal mix.

Myth of the male breadwinner—Based on the concept that the male is the stronger sex, this myth was designed to protect and provide for the weaker female in a society in which women had little or no power. This myth often causes women to be viewed as inferior to men and relegated to housekeeping and baby-sitting duties. Actually, the luxury of women staying at home while the man functioned as the only breadwinner is a rather recent innovation. During the three decades following World War II it was possible for some males to earn enough to provide for their family without assistance. A new invention called television portrayed Ozzie and Harriet Nelson as the ideal American family. Such family roles were often proclaimed by both clergy and society as natural and were even defended as being designed by God. Actually, such a narrow view of male/female roles or family is not found in Scripture. Rather than the female being suited only for housework and child rearing, the Bible provides a much broader concept of a woman's role, both in her family and society.

"A wife of noble character who can find? She is worth far more than rubies. Her husband has full confidence in her and lacks nothing of value. She brings him good, not harm, all the days of her life. She selects wool and flax and works with eager hands. She is like the merchant ships, bringing her food from afar. She gets up while it is still dark; she provides food for her family and portions for her servant girls. She considers a field and buys it; out of her earnings she plants a vineyard. She sets about her work vigorously; her arms are strong for her tasks. She sees that her trading is profitable, and her lamp does not go out at night. In her hand she holds the distaff and grasps the spindle with her fingers. She opens her arms to the poor and extends her hands to the needy. When it snows, she has no fear for her household; for all of them are clothed in scarlet. She makes coverings for her bed; she is clothed in fine linen and purple. Her husband is respected at the city gate, where he takes his seat among the elders of the land. She makes linen garments and sells them, and supplies the merchants with sashes. She is clothed with strength and dignity; she can laugh at the days to come. She speaks with wisdom, and faithful instruction is on her tongue. She watches over the affairs of her household and does not eat the bread of idleness. Her children arise and call her blessed; her husband also, and he praises her" (Prov. 31:10-28, NIV).

I get exhausted just reading her job description! From household manager to energetic entrepreneur, this biblical woman breaks the Ozzie and Harriet mold of the traditional family. In an agrarian society the entire family often worked from dawn to dusk. The structure of Old Testament families, designed as units of protection and survival, became distorted down through the centuries into specific categories of men's work and women's work. While many of these artificial cultural barriers have already been broken down by liberated women, few changes have been initiated by men because it is easier for men to maintain power when women do not have equal earning potential.

Myth of the blue-collar chauvinist—This myth depicts the blue-collar worker as compensating for his lack of material and social status by affirming his masculinity in outrageous ways. He is sometimes referred to as being a "redneck" or "good old boy." Archie Bunker in *All in the Family* was the stereotype of this myth. The male is seen as suspicious, complaining, selfish, and unloving except in unspoken ways. And Edith Bunker was stereotypically portrayed as flighty, slightly dim-witted, but heroically loving and loyal.

Recent surveys indicate that the opposite is actually true in blue-collar families. White-collar males perform an insignificant 5 percent of the housework, while blue-collar males accomplish four times more of the family chores. Although it may be true that the blue-collar male may swagger and boast a lot when he is with the "boys," he rarely acts like Archie Bunker at home.

Myth of the male Latin lover—The Latin male is supposedly more capable of intimate behavior than American and northern European males. Actually, the opposite is true. Latin men frequently have an exaggerated self-image, machismo, that tends to prevent true intimacy. Although a man's cultural background may influence his lovemaking style, it does not determine whether or not he is a great lover.

Both men and women tend to find comfort in these and other myths, since they tend to justify and perpetuate behavior that is familiar and does not require change.

Sexual Stages

Once aroused for sex during adolescence, the average male begins a journey of obsession. As previously mentioned, the average teenage male thinks of sex every three minutes. Not even sleep can detour his mind from sexual thoughts, and wet dreams become commonplace.

Locker rooms are too often the training centers for male sexuality. Sexual mysteries are revealed by slightly older boys rather than experienced men. Male sexuality is spoken of in crude terms designed to separate men from women. To be one of the "boys" the average teen begins to use four-letter words that shock adults but win the approval of his male peer group. Sexual experience elevates young males to the role of locker-room hero, much like the notches on a gunfighter's gun. Dur-

White-collar males perform an insignificant 5 percent of the housework, while blue-collar males accomplish four times more of the family chores.

ing this stage of life men become sexual "warriors," constantly seeking to engage the opposite sex in hand-to-hand, or more accurately, mouth-to-mouth and genital-to-genital combat.

Every locker room has four classes of sexual warriors. The most respected warriors are those with the most conquests, usually referred to as *studs* or make-out artists. Next are the *cheerleaders*, who applaud and encourage the studs to tell more tall tales. Too embarrassed to talk about sex are the *shy virgins*, who absorb information but seldom engage in conversation. Finally, there are the *silent lovers*, who already have a steady girlfriend whom they respect and love. The crude talk of the studs and cheerleaders turns them off, and they seldom pay much attention to locker-room bravado.

Fortunately, most of the locker-room bragging lacks any element of truth, but unfortunately, many of the teenage males do not realize it. Such bragging statements as "She was asking for it, so I gave it to her!" actually encourage date rape, which is often viewed as "satisfying a woman" by locker-room warriors. Some men remain forever in the locker room and fill their lives with date rape, porno magazines and films, backseat escapades, and one-night stands. These stilted, self-proclaimed studs view women merely as objects with desirable parts to be used or abused at will by the dominant male.

Eventually most males graduate from the locker room into the marriage bedroom. But how do warriors change their behavior from conquest to caring, from scoring to making love, from irresponsible stud to monogamous husband? Fortunately many males switch from sexual warrior to sexual *worker* when they enter the marriage bed. While they are no longer constantly seeking conquests, they now must prove themselves a consistent sexual worker capable of satisfying their mate for a lifetime. Unfortunately, the locker room has not prepared most men for this task.

"Traditionally, the sexual tests of manhood were not genital. A 'real' man proved himself by impregnating a woman, protecting her against enemies, and providing for his family. Currently, easily available birth control and the desire for small families or childless marriages have removed the fertility test; unpopular wars and nuclear arms have eroded the conviction that we are being protected by the military; and two-career families have taken away the male role of being the provider. As a consequence, men seem enormously invested in pleasing and performing for women. For many men the erogenous zones seem to have replaced the battlefield as the arena for testing of manhood" (Sam Keen, *Fire in the Belly: On Being a Man*, p. 76).

Most men today feel it is their responsibility to satisfy their mate sexually but are fearful of revealing their feelings to their spouse. While many liberated women have taken responsibility for their own sexual enjoyment and no longer wait passively for the male to "hit the right spot," few women have bothered to inform the men of their decision. Most men still feel frustrated or a failure if they cannot bring their wife to orgasm. Sensing this insecurity in the male, more than half of all married women fake orgasm on occasion. Unfortunately, most men feel there is only one correct way to be sexual: erect and in control. Men often feel obligated to perform, and this obsession sometimes drives them to have sex outside the marriage just to make sure the "equipment" is still functioning properly.

Whether or not men are biologically monogamous has been the source of much conjecture, but it really is not a relevant question, because masculine behavior has been distorted throughout the centuries by cultural conditioning. Today's average male certainly does not compare to God's original model in physique, personality, or sexuality. Centuries of sexual distortions and masculine myths have made it very difficult for men to determine who or what they ought to be today. One study revealed that four out of 10 happily married men reported erectile or ejaculatory dysfunction, and one out of two reported a lack of interest in their mate (Herb Goldberg, *The New Male-Female Relationship*, p. 75).

The combination of male myths, cultural conditioning, and social stress has created male resentment toward women. Men who were taught to be sexual warriors (initiators) as well as sexual workers (satisfiers) feel it is their duty to initiate sex and often feel guilty when it is unsatisfactory. Women sometimes compound the problem by failing to understand the importance of sex to the male psyche. Worse yet, some women view this male obsession as animalistic, degrading, and downright dirty because they have been culturally conditioned in an opposite direction.

Men begin to feel manipulated by women who dangle their sexuality as a prize or reward, and often resent having to read a woman's mind and then being penalized when they read it wrong. This reinforces their locker-room training that sex is a bestowed favor and has little or nothing to do with intimacy.

To the sexual warrior and worker, a woman's sexuality is *paradise* to be obtained. Much of a man's life is focused on finding his way into the *promised land*. Many men willingly accept their role as provider and protector, but they also expect some reward for their lifetime of struggle and toil. Men look to women to make them feel whole and reconnect them to feelings that fathers and locker rooms have taken away. Through the sexual act men seek to enter *paradise lost*, and the penis becomes the bridge that once again connects them to their true feelings, even if only for a moment.

However, to the sexual warrior/worker, women also represent judgment. Entrance into paradise depends on not offending the keepers of the gates. Men give women power to judge, reward, or punish them at will because of the male obsession with sex. Therefore, men set out to fulfill women's demands with the expectation of receiving a reward or at least avoiding punishment. Eventually some men begin to view this as a slave/master relationship and feel resentful. Worse yet, men may even begin to judge themselves through the condemning reflection in the eyes of a judgmental mate.

There is a fundamental difference between male and female sexuality. Men imagine sex directly and intimacy indirectly, whereas women imagine intimacy directly and sex indirectly. As warriors and workers men have been culturally conditioned to view sex as the *only* legitimate way to feel close to another human being. Warriors and workers are conditioned that it is not acceptable to admit or express feelings. The male role that most men are taught is to stand and deliver. Men want sex, and women want relationships. Men want flesh, and women want love.

Actually, sex begins in the male brain and not in his penis. High concentrations of testosterone, acting on the male brain, mediated through the hypothalamus, cause the average man to be more sexually active (both in actions and imagination) than the average woman. Adolescent males mastur-

> **When men look to sex as the source of male identity, it becomes a futile search. Sex may bring pleasure or joy, but it does not provide identity.**

bate more frequently, seek sexual gratification more frequently, and even though maturing later, have sexual intercourse at an earlier age than girls. Men, deprived of sex, are much more likely to become morose and irritable—women rarely experience the same feeling of deprivation in a celibate state. Women who are celibate miss the companionship of sex, while men miss *sex*!

When men look to sex as the source of male identity, it becomes a futile search. Sex may bring pleasure or joy, but it does not provide identity. Contrary to popular opinion, men are not a life-support system for their penises. Cultural conditioning and modern sexual rites of manhood provide a constant source of irritation, contention, and stress between the sexes. In other words, cultural conditioning drives both men and women crazy. The two sexes are taught to speak different sexual languages and also to complain because they don't understand each other. Men and women are conditioned to expect impossible things from one another and then blame each other for a lack of fulfillment.

Date rape, sexual harassment, and modern divorce statistics are all indicators of a male identity crisis created by their culture, parents, and peers. For example, parents unknowingly teach boy babies to perform by picking them up less frequently than the female infant when they cry. As a result, the average boy by the age of 13 months is more likely to tough it out and refrain from crying than the average girl. Boys quickly become comfortable solving their own problems by *doing* rather than complaining or crying. In addition, the suppression of feelings is taught to male children from early childhood as the norm for masculinity. Is it any wonder that many men grow up to be insensitive, self-centered, egotistical, "I-can-do-it-myself," domineering warriors ready to conquer and exploit?

Boys are also taught that there is a price tag on female sexuality. Culture, parents, and older peers teach adolescent males to pick up the tab if they want to attract someone of the opposite sex. Rather than receiving a dowry (like in Old Testament times) for marrying a woman, modern males spend a fortune trying to attract their future lover. One man in a male group confessed: "It was the senior prom. I took her to dinner at Alfredo's, and a formal Italian waiter handed me a wine list. I was so insecure that I actually ordered a bottle, even though neither of us drank alcohol. It cost me $10. That meant mowing our lawn once a week for a month to impress her with a bottle of wine that neither of us drank. What with dinner, dessert, coffee, tax, and tip, the whole thing ran over $60. It took me six months to earn that money. I also got her an orchid; my tuxedo, prom tickets, and gas for the car. Wow! Another $60. Oh yeah. Then we went up to this neat place after the prom to get a view of the city and of course we had to have something to drink, so all together it cost me more than $150. And that was 30 years ago" (adapted from Warren Farrell, *Why Men Are the Way They Are*, pp. 122, 123).

Culture has taught men to view these expenditures as an investment in their sexual future. Is it any wonder that some men begin to view women as objects that are purchased for a price?

Men are taught early in adolescence that if they don't initiate, women won't. What little sex is available goes to those bold enough to ask. Therefore, the average man must be prepared to risk rejection 100 times in order to be successful once. The emotional price that men pay for sex is irrational, obsessive, and out of proportion with real life. Men learn to risk everything for a woman, including their careers, financial investments, and even their lives. In addition, men are taught to sacrifice themselves for the sake of a woman. One often reads of men risking their lives to save a woman or of women sacrificing themselves to save a child, but how often do you read of a woman risking her life for a man? Women seldom risk their lives for men because our culture has declared it an inappropriate response in the male/female game plan.

Sexual roles are more than a game in the American culture. For the male, success is important, and sex is often the first testing ground outside the playground. In pursuit of a woman he will develop and perfect a strategy that he will employ in factories or boardrooms for the rest of his life. Successful men are those who take the responsibility for turning *nos* into *yeses*. Therefore, in order to be considered a success with women, a man attempts to discover which *nos* really mean no, which *nos* mean maybe, and which *nos* are really the occasional yes. Men who follow this formula for success (i.e., that a *no* really does not mean no) will later discover whether they have been lovers or rapists.

Men are taught that women give subtle clues that need interpretation. After all, reasons a man, if a woman really does not want sex, she should give a clear, unmistakable signal that needs no interpretation. Short of a karate punch to the throat or an attention-getting kick to the groin, he hears her really saying, "Convince me. I'm still listening."

Clear communication is further hindered because culture conditions women to hint or suggest rather than to command or proclaim. In addition, if a woman truly likes a man, she may give more subtle clues to stop in order to protect his fragile ego.

Sexual roles are more than a game in the American culture.

Male/female communication styles can sometimes create the conditions for date rape, domination, abuse, and other violence.

Men learn early in their experience that it hurts less to be rejected by a sex object than to be rejected by a human being. Therefore, many men conveniently turn women into an object and sex into a game that must be won. The purpose of the game is to *score*. He who scores the most is the winner of the male identity award. Warriors and workers both compete. Competition is what male life is all about! The rules of this cultural game divide the female body into objective parts that must be conquered one at a time in order to obtain paradise. The usual progression for the sexual warrior/worker is to start at the top of the woman's body and work down.

> *Men are often mistaken about the sexual intentions of a woman touching him. Once a man discovers that a woman isn't interested in him, he is more likely to feel deceived rather than merely rejected.*

Constantly tuned in to the sexual channel in their brain, men are likely to mistake friendliness by a woman as having sexual overtones (Bucknell University study, *Men's Health*, October 1991, p. 15). Men are often mistaken about the sexual intentions of a woman touching him. Once a man discovers that a woman isn't interested in him, he's more likely to feel deceived rather than merely rejected. Men become so focused on obtaining paradise that they find it difficult to go slow in a relationship, and if a woman initiates sex, it becomes almost impossible for a man to say no. How can one say no to paradise when it is offered?

Culture also teaches men to suppress their real feelings in a relationship and replace them with dishonest clichés to elicit the desired response. Men learn that total honesty in a relationship with a woman is often a disaster. If a man tells a woman early in a relationship that he finds her body sexually attractive, he fears that she will reject him. So he suppresses his true feelings, which are often unacceptable to the woman, and tells her what she wants to hear. Men learn early in life that most relationships are best started with a degree of dishonesty.

According to the male culture, it is more important to have frequent sex than quality sex. Male talk often assumes that no man is getting more sex than he wants. Even if a man was getting too much sex (surveys indicate about 1 percent of males complain of this), he usually will be reluctant to admit it for fear of being considered a wimp. Locker-room bravado demands a constant complaining about the lack of sex and an arrogant attitude designed to focus on the task and not on feelings. The male emphasis upon frequency may cover up fears of inadequacies in his own love-making ability. After all, if a man constantly complains about the lack of sex, no one can fault him for the poor quality of sex.

Success is often viewed as the male insurance policy against rejection both in the boardroom and in the bedroom. Success is defined as a man's ability to turn *nos* and *maybes* into *yeses*. Therefore, all of life becomes a contest of wills in sports, careers, and sex. Men are taught only one way to play a game and that is to *win*! Success means never taking no for an answer and giving 110 percent at all times. Power becomes both an addictive high and the ultimate aphrodisiac to attract women. The male attitude of success at any price is both admired and hated by women in the boardroom and the bedroom.

The bottom line is that men are culturally conditioned with specific sexual attitudes early in life. Men become almost addicted to sex because it is seen as being in short supply. The law of supply and demand is part of the female cultural training, teaching her that sex can be traded for money, security, status, and power in a male-dominated society. As women begin to take more equal roles in society, this female myth may soon be put aside. Because the demand exceeds the supply, men are conditioned to risk constant rejection and even humiliation in order to obtain sex. So powerful is this conditioning that men frequently turn women into sex objects, which is often a defense against entering into a truly intimate relationship for which he has not been culturally prepared. So complete is this cultural conditioning that some men even treat their wives as objects. The male competitive nature, conditioned by culture, creates a multitude of male/female problems in the area of sexuality and relationships.

Contrary to what most men have been conditioned to believe, it is perfectly permissible for a man to say no to sex. Women are taught early in childhood to say no, but most men have little training in that area. Many men are so obsessed with sex that it would never occur to them to say no. Actually, men, like women, are entitled to choose the time or place rather than perpetuate the myth of the ever-ready stud. Just as more women become comfortable with initiating sex, so men must become comfortable with saying no. If a man cannot say no to sex, it means someone else is ruling over his body. This is not acceptable for either male or female. Some men use Paul's counsel to the Corinthian church as justification for having sex with their wives upon demand. "The husband should fulfill his marital duty to his wife, and likewise the wife to her husband. The wife's body does not belong to her alone but also to her husband. In the same way, the husband's body does not belong to him alone but also to his wife. Do not deprive each other except by mutual consent and for a time, so that you may devote yourselves to prayer. Then come together again so that Satan will not tempt you because of your lack of self-control. I say this as a concession, not as a command" (1 Cor. 7:3-6, NIV).

Paul is referring to the practice of abstinence and even celibacy among some married couples in a misguided attempt to gain special status in the kingdom of God. In addition, Paul recognizes that sex has been used as a weapon in the war between the sexes throughout recorded history. With this in

Women are taught early in childhood to say no, but most men have little training in that area. Many men are so obsessed with sex that it would never occur to them to say no.

mind, he asks the Corinthian church members to lay down their sexual weapons and concentrate on strengthening the *one flesh* relationship. Paul's bottom line is that every married person should put the spouse *first*. Studies have shown that couples who each initiate and refuse sex equally have more frequent sex and are happier with their sex lives and their whole relationship than couples who do not achieve this equality (Astrachan, *How Men Feel*, p. 272).

Mutual consideration and respect is the point of Paul's admonition, which was in direct contrast to the chattel-property concept that was (and often still is) a popular view toward women in marital relationships. So, men, Paul did not issue a biblical insurance policy for sex upon demand. Instead, he treated men and women as equal sexual beings with mutual needs and desires.

Ron and Karen Flowers offer an enlightening explanation of male-female equality in the Garden of Eden: "Adam slept while God created the woman. Because a rib from his side supplied the substance from which God fashioned her, the two parts of humanity have a common origin, the same earthy raw material (cf. Gen. 2:7; 3:19). One is not superior to the other. Eden knows no competition, no disharmony, no inequality. The creation from the rib makes a symbolic statement. Writes Ellen White, echoing an old rabbinical tradition, 'Eve was created from a rib taken from the side of Adam, signifying that she was not to control him as the head, nor to be trampled under his feet as an inferior, but to stand by his side as an equal, to be loved and protected by him'" (*Love Aflame*, p. 78).

The idea that the male sex drive, once set in motion, cannot be stopped or brought under control is also a myth. Men continue to perpetuate this myth because it means that they are not responsible for their actions once they have become aroused sexually. This myth has even been expanded in certain cultures to include anger. If an abuser or killer is controlled by the emotion of anger, then he is not responsible for his actions. Contrary to these popular myths, men can learn to control the outward expression of both their sex drive and anger.

Men should also note that females possess a sex drive of their own that is just waiting to be discovered and enjoyed by a sensitive and understanding male. When a woman initiates sex, it is sometimes threatening to the male if he happens to view such initiation as his prerogative alone. More reliable birth control methods have made it possible for women to discover their own sexual thresholds and to seek sexual pleasure without fear of pregnancy. Current research reveals that most men view penetration as a necessity for having sex. However, penetration is usually not the key that unlocks a woman's sexual response. Because today's woman is viewed as a more informed consumer (whether or not she really is), the uninformed male is often intimidated and may even become sexually dysfunctional.

Male dominance is the result of sin and not part of God's original design. If the goal of salvation is to restore Eden lost, then Christians need to return to Edenic mutuality in male/female relationships. Dominance, power, and control in a Christian home actually lift up humanity's sins rather than Christ's cross. Jesus' admonition to love your neighbor as yourself applies directly to the male/female relationship and not just to one's friends or neighbors. Men who have been conditioned by culture to take power for granted and suppress their feelings can, and must, change. Expressions of feelings and mutual acceptance in the area of sex not only make a marriage relationship more enjoyable, but also provide a glimpse of Eden restored.

Since sexuality is 99 percent perception and less than 1 percent performance, it is more profitable for men to concentrate on understanding their perceptions and feelings than to try to improve their performance. Scripture reveals a basic psychological law that applies to male sexuality: "For as he [a man] thinks in his heart, so is he" (Prov. 23:7, NKJV).

The Best-kept Male Secret!

Doctors estimate that 10 million American men currently suffer from chronic impotence. That is one out of every 11 men! Tragically, much of it goes untreated because of a combination of fear, ignorance, and shame on the part of men. Actually, male impotency is not only treatable, but is highly curable.

Any man who fails to achieve an erection during a period of weeks or months should see a doctor. Approximately 64 percent of men put off a doctor's visit for a year or more because they are afraid to discuss sexual dysfunction openly with a physician. It is not uncommon for some men to wait up to 10

> **Doctors estimate that 10 million American men currently suffer from chronic impotence. Tragically, much of it goes untreated because of a combination of fear, ignorance, and shame on the part of men. Actually, male impotency is not only treatable, but is highly curable.**

years before going for a physical exam (*Men's Health*, October 1991, p. 14). It is encouraging to note that most men can be treated effectively with counseling, drug or hormone injections, or erection-enhancing devices, and that fewer than 10 percent will actually require surgery. Impotency is triggered by physical and psychological problems. It is important for a man to have a complete physical exam before counseling, since approximately half of all impotency has a physical origin. If the problem is psychological, counseling offers dramatic help in most cases.

There is no commanding evidence that the feminist movement has increased the occurrence of impotency. A lack of statistics and records from the past century makes it difficult to research. However, it is important to note that the United States Patent Office granted 96 patents for inventions regarding genitalia from 1887 to 1975. The vast majority of these patents granted through the 1950s were intended to create or maintain erections. Evidently impotency is not a recent problem created by the feminist movement. It is true that impotency has many causes today that were relatively unknown a few generations ago. Increased drug and alcohol consumption, longer life spans, and increased use of prescription medications can create impotency. Something as simple as changing to another prescription often cures the problem. More aggressive and sometimes insensitive females can trigger feelings of inadequacy in some males—sort of like the bashful bladder syndrome except that it applies to an erection. Today's fast pace, with its ever-increasing demands and pressures, can create sexual dysfunction. In addition, more men than in the past are seeking help now. It is important to note that impotency does not indicate a lack of maleness any more than menopause indicates a lack of femaleness.

Fear of impotency or the inability to have an erection upon command may cause some elderly men to consider retiring from sexual activities when they retire from their career. While this may be a valid choice for some men, it is definitely not mandatory to retire sexually just because you are no longer a part of the rat race. Actually, retirement years can provide opportunity for the most meaningful sex of a lifetime, because the couple has time to spend with each other. Our society often labels an elderly man who is interested in sex as a "dirty old man," and adult children sometimes view their parents' normal sexual urges as embarrassing or degrading. Even grown children have been known to put obstacles in the path of their parents in an attempt to discourage them from having sex.

Some aging men are convinced that their sexual interests are inappropriate for someone their age. As they look in the mirror at their deteriorating body, some fear that their mates will no longer find them attractive. Other senior citizens were raised with the Victorian concept that sex is

Actually, retirement years can provide opportunity for the most meaningful sex of a lifetime, because the couple has time to spend with each other.

dirty and a tool of the devil.

With all these culturally conditioned doubts and negative feelings about themselves, some older men become convinced that they are not adequate lovers, so they simply give up on sex, claiming to be too old or too sick for such things. This behavior is sometimes triggered by a *temporary* erection failure that leaves them too embarrassed and traumatized to try again. Other older men find it a relief no longer to be designated as workers or warriors and willingly lay down their earlier obsession to perform sexually. For these men sex had become just one more job to perform with few rewards and lots of disappointments. Once a man feels that sex is a command performance rather than a mutually enjoyable act, he's not far from sexual retirement.

Problem: Giving up on sex often dispenses with *all* forms of physical affection for fear that one's partner will want more. A man often feels uncomfortable starting something he fears he cannot finish.

Solution: There are no biological or medical reasons for sexual retirement, only a lot of cultural conditioning and myths that cause many older people unnecessary pain and misery. If a man decides he wants to remain sexually active, there is usually no reason to stop. However, if he decides sex is not for him, it is still important for him to maintain physical contact with his spouse. The choice belongs to the man, not to society. "Norton was 76. He had enjoyed a good sexual relationship with his wife for over 40 years but then had a few erection failures and assumed that he was over the hill. For almost 10 years he hadn't tried to have sex with his spouse.

"He and his wife still engaged in some physical contact, but not as much as before, because he didn't want to lead her on. After reading an article about sex and aging in a popular magazine, he decided to see if anything could be done.

"He had all the usual, narrow ideas about sex, as did his wife. Intercourse had always been the culmination of their sexual activity, and they could barely think of anything that could be done without an erection.

"But they had a very close and warm relationship and were able to look at new models of sex. It took only a few weeks for them to resume satisfying sexual activity.

"Here is what he said in his last therapy session: 'I guess it's never too late to teach an old dog some new tricks. I haven't had so much fun in a long time. And to think of all the time we wasted because I was so fired up with concern about an erection. It comes around pretty good now, but like you said, not every time. But that's all right, I don't need it every time.

"'I just like to play around with Emmy, and she loves it. I haven't seen this much fire in her eyes for 20 years or more. And when she plays with me, it's just like I was back in high school again. Wow, I just want to eat her up.

"'It's really good to be back with her again like this. And I don't intend to stop, ever'" (*Men's Health*, February 1991, p. 9).

CHAPTER 7

Mr. Dad!

A man in Oklahoma was cleaning the house while his wife was shopping. Decked out with his cleaning apron, he was busy vacuuming when he heard the doorbell ring. Pulling the vacuum with him to the door, he was confronted by a burly ranch foreman with a battered cowboy hat pulled low over his eyes, faded jeans, and worn boots.

"I was just cleaning the house for my wife," the homeowner offered in a weak and apologetic voice.

Looking relieved, the rancher replied gruffly, "I understand completely. I'm delivering Avon!"

How times have changed since I (Len) was a boy! The thought of my father vacuuming or delivering Avon was incongruous with his perceived role as a man. Quite frankly, real men didn't do housework and certainly never delivered Avon—at least they would never admit it to their peers if they did. But we live in a different world today. Ozzie and Harriet left suburbia 30 years ago, and their home has since been owned by a two-income family, a single parent with two children, and most recently by a working mother and unemployed father. Today's family configurations are challenging to the typical male, who may have been brought up to view child rearing as a feminine responsibility.

The old saying that boys are a "chip off the old block" is often a perpetuated truism by the transfer of information and misinformation from one generation to the next. We learn how to be fathers from our fathers. One wonders how long God must have prepared Adam to be a father, since Adam was 130 years old when Seth was born. The first two sons (Cain and Abel) didn't work out too well, and it would be Seth's responsibility to continue the family lineage. Scripture records that Adam "became the father of a son in his own likeness, after his image, and named him Seth" (Gen. 5:3, RSV). We do create sons in our own image. From our fathers we learn the good, the bad, and the ugly and transfer that same information to our sons. From Adam came not only Cain and Abel, but also Seth.

Fathers are a paradox to their sons. Their sons both love them and hate them. They bond with them and form barriers to prevent intimacy. They share in both camaraderie and competition. Inevitably, a power struggle is brought on by feelings of inferiority in the son and emotional distance

Most father-son relations go through stages of reverence, revolt, and eventual reconciliation.

by the father. Most father-son relations go through stages of reverence, revolt, and eventual reconciliation.

Fathers are often not all they appear to be at first glance by a child. To the small child a father is initially a *hero* who later may be viewed as a *hoax* before finally becoming a *healer*. Father-son relationships are a microcosm of how males often relate to each other. Men do not simply enter manhood; they must earn it. A rite of passage separates men from their parents and from their fathers in particular. Only then can they join the brotherhood of *men*. The final rite of passage usually involves their relationship with their father.

A man in his late 50s confessed to me that when his father died it was as if a heavy weight had been lifted from his shoulders. This man had been 51 when his father passed away. "I loved my father," he cried, searching for words, "but I never felt like I measured up to his expectations of me, even though I earned two master's degrees and a Ph.D. He was always there, judging my work, even when he lived several states away."

For many men life is a long search for a reunion with their lost fathers. The Homeric *Odyssey* includes Telemachus' hunt for his father, Ulysses. More recently, the *Star Wars* anthology was about Luke Skywalker seeking to avenge his father's death, only to discover that his archenemy, Darth Vader, was actually his father. Even when the father has not left home, he may be lost to his son in a maze of other responsibilities and distorted ideas about fatherhood.

Most lessons are transmitted nonverbally from father to son. Early in life a son begins to imitate his father's behavior. After all, dad is his hero. The first lesson that most sons learn relates to *power*. This lesson is usually transmitted more by example than by words. Perhaps the earliest lesson is that fathers have power and sons do not. In order to achieve power, the son must be like the father. In order to be like the father, the son must eventually usurp the father's power.

Sons learn that power is often a determiner of relationships. Dad is bigger and stronger. Dad has power over the children. Dad controls the flow of money, where they go on vacation, which car they buy, and even how Mom spends her time.

If it wasn't so tragic, the experience of two parents looking through their wedding album with their little girl would be humorous. Suddenly the daughter pointed to the pictures and exclaimed, "Daddy, is that the day you got Mommy to come and work for us?"

That question reveals how power is silently transmitted to children through parental relationships.

Many times the house schedule revolves around the father's comings and goings (mostly goings). Most children view their fathers' workplaces as shadowy realms to which they hurry off in the morning and from which they return tired out and grumpy at the end

One day as a young mother and her 5-year-old son were driving down the street, the inquisitive little boy asked a revealing question, "Mommy, why do the idiots only come out when Daddy drives?"

of the day. In addition, father knows everything (at least that's what he tells the family), so there's no way to argue with him.

One day as a young mother and her 5-year-old son were driving down the street, the inquisitive little boy asked a revealing question, "Mommy, why do the idiots only come out when Daddy drives?"

A son cannot compete with his father or do as well as he does, so he often feels inferior to him—even at the age of 51. Fathers are our first male oppressors. We learn how to oppress others by observing our fathers. The lessons of power begin very early in childhood and surely shape the male's concept of manhood.

For many men, being a man means to conceal the worrisome traces of an inner life and to deny any emotion except anger. Real men do not weep or express fear. Real men express anger and take charge.

The second lesson we learn from our fathers is *self-reliance*. The hallmark of being a male is said to be emotional aloofness. A lawyer describes his father's lack of emotions: "He was totally incapable of showing feelings, and it wasn't even a question of rational choice for him. My mother says that he would show her affection by sometimes doing the housework, since he had more energy than she did, but otherwise, he didn't show anyone a thing. He couldn't even call my mother by her name; he called her 'mother' instead, and when the time came, he called her 'grandma.' She would really plead with him to use her name, but he just couldn't do it. He was just so uptight about his feelings. He was such a tight person that even calling her by her name made him nervous" (Donald Bell, *Being a Man: The Paradox of Masculinity*, p. 17).

For many men, being a man means to conceal the worrisome traces of an inner life and to deny any emotion except anger. Real men do not weep or express fear. Real men express anger and take charge. Man-to-man talks seldom take place except in the movies. Such attempts usually degenerate into a monologue or dissertation by the father on how the son should live his life.

"The only time Dad ever really talked to me was when I was living at home, in college, and into my first heavy relationship with a girl. I was coming home late a lot, and as I stole through the front door at four one morning, Dad came out of his bedroom and took me aside. He said he was concerned about me and we should talk later. We went out to lunch the next day, but he never mentioned the previous night. It wasn't necessary for him to spout off about what was bugging him; just knowing I was keeping him up nights was enough to make me want to mend my ways" (*Men's Health*, June 1991, p. 81).

Stages of Fatherhood

The first stage of fatherhood is that of *hero*. To a young boy, father is a giant from whose shoulders the world can be viewed safely.

To a young boy, father is superman. All-powerful! His interest in violent contact sports reinforces the emotionless, competitive, traditional male character handed down from generation to generation. Fathers can move mountains, or at least excel as Monday morning quarterbacks.

Hero-dad can solve any problem. "My father repeatedly told me and my three brothers, 'Whatever you can conceive and believe, you can achieve.' I heard it so often I actually believe it today" (*ibid.*, June 1991, p. 81).

One glance from hero-dad can heal—or create a hurt.

"On my fourth birthday, my dad took me to Freedomland, a Wild West amusement park in the vast uncharted wilderness somewhere east of the Pecos and west of Fair Lawn, New Jersey. The last attraction of the day was a stagecoach ride, but what began as a pleasant little jaunt soon turned scary when we were bushwhacked by a band of outlaws. They chased us, hooves pounding and guns blazing. Finally, they overtook us, pulled the coach to a stop, threw open the door, and held us up at gunpoint.

"Naturally, I assumed they were after my special issue Freedomland souvenir tricolor pen, so I did what any self-respecting 4-year-old would have done—I cried like a banshee. It was then that my father performed the most remarkable act of bravery I'd ever seen. He looked the gang leader right in the eyes and said, 'All right, fellas. That's enough.'

"To my astonishment, that ruthless desperado looked back at my father and mumbled, 'OK. Sorry, sir.' Then he and his cutthroat gang holstered their six-shooters and hightailed it for the hills. The world was once again safe. My dad was a hero. I never forgot the feeling it gave me, and I hope I can make my son feel that way about me someday" (*ibid.*).

It is during this time of hero-worship that fathers often absent themselves from fatherhood. Playing the role of the greatest, biggest, and best is too heavy for some fathers to carry. Lost fathers withdraw into their work under the guise of doing it for their family. Some substitute gifts to make up for lost time with their family. Others withdraw emotionally and physically, and the son feels abandoned and betrayed. Sons expect the same from other men and learn to withdraw into their own unemotional shell, which will protect them.

Paul Tsongas, a senator (later a presidential candidate), learned that he had cancer. His condition caused him to reevaluate the time he had been spending with his wife and children compared with the time he spent at work. After enjoying a rare evening at home with his family, he realized that with the schedule he was keeping, the next night like this would be several years in the future. After such a sobering realization, he made this observation: "Nobody on his deathbed ever said, 'I wish I had spent more time on my job.'"

Hero-dad may also be a stranger whom some sons

> **"Nobody on his deathbed ever said, 'I wish I had spent more time on my job.'"**

never quite get to know. I cannot remember my father ever holding me, although I'm told that he did. One recent study indicates that 50 percent of men cannot recall being hugged by their fathers. My father didn't have time to play with me. I assume that it was because he was a farmer and that there was always too much work to do. As I got older he taught me how to hunt by going with me three or four times. He taught me never to shoot anything I didn't intend to eat. Later he taught me how to drive a car by going with me two or three times. When I turned 14 he bought me a car. I know it was his way of saying he loved me

Absent fathers leave permanent scars. Fathers who withdraw their emotions tend to foster the same pattern in their sons. Fathers who withdraw their physical presence may actually influence the social behavior of their sons.

and was proud of me, but I sure wish he could have told me in person or hugged me more as a child.

Where was my hero-dad when I was a little boy? Why didn't he have time to play with me? Where was he when I wanted to play at his feet or sit on his shoulders? I have a picture of me sitting on his shoulders once. It is mocking evidence of the only time I can recall doing this. The role of hero was transferred to my grandfather and uncle. They shared with me the time my father never seemed to have.

Absent fathers leave permanent scars. Fathers who withdraw their emotions tend to foster the same pattern in their sons. Fathers who withdraw their physical presence may actually influence the social behavior of their sons. Studies indicate that sons of lost fathers are less assertive, more dependent, more submissive, and less secure in their role as a man. Gang culture is society's method of filling the void left by the absentee father. One study of 300 seventh and eighth graders asked them to keep a careful record of the time they spent alone with their fathers during a two-week period. The average boy in the study spent seven and a half minutes alone with his father each week.

"The conflict of who the father appears to be and who he really is plagues a boy trying to learn to become a man. Not only does he receive mixed messages, but he suffers supreme disappointment and frustration in investing so much hope and trust—so much love and pride—in a hero who seems, through his silence, to be rejecting the boy" (Perry Garfinkle, *In a Man's World*, p. 20).

Why is it so difficult for fathers to tell their sons, "I love you"?

During a male retreat, the participants were asked to complete this thought, When I think of my father I feel . . . Here are some of the responses:

• hurt, rejected, half a man.

• a strange distance and confusion about his actual role in my life and a fear that somehow or other I have learned to react in ways he reacts, and I feel trapped by it or him.

• separate, angry, rejected, scared that he's going to die before I get what I want from him. On rare occasions I feel love.

• I had such a weak experience with my father that I would like to compensate for it by being good to my children, and I've taken that as the most important mission in my life.

Another question, If my father were here I'd say to him . . . , brought equally candid replies.

• I don't know what I'd say to him. I've never been able to approach him, and I don't think I could start now.

• "Old man, why don't you cross the street? Why don't you take a risk?"

• "Dad, why don't you come out? You seem so bottled up inside, and I get hurt by that. I can't reach you, and it's frustrating."

• [*crying*] "Dad, I just want to say I love you."

Why is it so difficult for fathers to tell their sons, "I love you"? "From the beginning, fatherhood is an awkward role to play. Biology forces men, taught from childhood to be active, into an unfamiliar and uncomfortable, even embarrassing passivity. After planting the seed, they take a backseat in the process, watching their wives balloon up. Pregnancy is a woman's journey, a mystery of creation men can never fathom. Men hear about the effects of pregnancy—the nausea, back pains, altered chemistry, altered physiology, altered moods—and they can commiserate, but never experience them. From the start of the process, they feel one step removed" (*ibid.*, p. 22).

The second stage of fatherhood is usually to be the *enemy*. Sons learn that the first duty of manhood is a declaration of independence. It is much easier to rebel against an enemy than a hero. Mark Twain summed it up quite well when he wrote: "When I was a boy of 14 my father was so ignorant I could hardly stand to have the old man around. But when I got to be 21 I was astonished at how much the old man had learned in those seven years."

A declaration of independence is especially important if the greatness of the father is overshadowing the son. The son may not be able to grow in his shadow. When I turned 15 there was a tremendous power struggle between my father and myself. We argued over the momentous issues of life such as hair length, curfew, and my work habits (or lack of them). By the time I turned 16 I was spending more time away from home than I was at home. The car my father had given me at 14 had provided me with mobility, and I fantasized about making it on my own. I didn't want to follow in my father's footsteps. I wanted to create my own path. He felt that I was degrading him and proclaiming that his life's work was not important. Our relationship fractured badly. Finally, he signed the papers for me to join the Air Force at the age of 17. I needed my independence to become a man. Unfortunately, the fractured relationship never fully healed.

Even if a son decides to follow in his father's footsteps, he will usually attempt to pass him on his path to success. Beating Dad at his own game is another form of rebellion and separation that is all part of becoming independent. For some, the process is never completed.

The next stage of fatherhood is *friend*. For many men, the struggle to come out from under the shadow of their fathers takes a positive turn when they too become fathers. I (Len) worried that my son might find it intimidating to compete with me in the same college. Since I started college at the age of 32, my son would have to attend the same classes fewer than seven years later. How would he feel having to compete with my 4.0? Would he feel inferior? Pressured? Angry? I'm happy to report that he created his own path through college and even worked for one of my favorite professors as a reader-aide. Ultimately he chose a different direction in both lifestyle and career.

No matter how old fathers become, their sons still feel like little boys in their presence. It's as though the sons stopped growing, in comparison to their fathers, at the age of 7. My very best male friend on this earth is my son, Mitch. I can talk to him about my successes and failures, my dreams and aspirations, and anything else that comes to mind. We support each other in time of need. We share candidly. He has seen me at both my best and my worst. Through it all he still calls me Dad, even though we have a deep and meaningful friendship. I try very hard not to play the role of power-dad and interfere with his life, but I must confess that I really love it when he calls me Dad.

The final stage of fatherhood—and final rite of passage—is the *death* of the father. Some men become angry when their fathers die, because they are abandoning them once again. Others feel guilty by the realization of their repressed death wish in order to get out from under his domineering control. Others feel fearful

> **No matter how old fathers become, their sons still feel like little boys in their presence.**

because they are now on their own and must prove themselves as men and fathers. No matter what the reaction to their father's death, most men feel that they have now attained the full stature of a man.

With the death of Father comes the responsibility to become family elder or patriarch. Sons must now show that they can indeed fill Father's shoes.

When "Pistol Pete" Maravich was inducted into the Basketball Hall of Fame he shared some poignant thoughts about his father. (Ironically, "Pistol Pete" died shortly after receiving this honor and sharing his testimony.) "These memories of Dad's goals for me were so clear on February 5, 1987, as I sat on a platform in Springfield, Massachusetts, surrounded by the most revered of all basketball achievers. Ironically, I once had told Dad back in my college days that if I ever made the Hall of Fame, I would refuse the award and tell them they had given it to the wrong guy. 'Give the award to my dad,' I had told him I'd say, 'because there is no way in the world I deserve the honor before he does.'

"As I look back now I finally feel as though I understand my inheritance. Dad handed me something beautiful and precious, and I will always be indebted to him. He gave me his life full of instruction and encouragement. He gave me hope in hopeless situations and laughter in the face of grim circumstances. Dad gave me an example of discipline unequaled, dedication unmatched. He gave me the privilege of seeing an unwavering faith when the darkness of life and death surrounded him. But, more than anything, my father became a symbol of what love and compassion can do in anyone's life, and I am happy to accept that love as his heir to a dream" (*Parables, Etc.*, April 1990, p. 3).

The New Fatherhood

Everything is changing! Our fathers did not prepare us for the altered circumstances men face today. "In a world which is changing rapidly and in which the expectations of men and women have dramatically shifted, the lessons our fathers taught us and the models of masculinity that they provided are often unacceptable. They conflict directly with new images of masculinity and femininity, with changing sex roles, and with emerging views of a man's place in the world" (Bell, p. 8).

The traditional reluctance of fathers to share in the sweat, toil, and tears of child care has fostered many negative results. This reluctance helped estrange us from our fathers, helped perpetuate the lost father, and put undue burden and stress upon women as mothers and nurturers. Many men today feel suspended somewhere between what their fathers taught them and

> *The traditional reluctance of fathers to share in the sweat, toil, and tears of child care has fostered many negative results. This reluctance helped estrange us from our fathers, helped perpetuate the lost father, and put undue burden and stress upon women as mothers and nurturers.*

what they have learned for themselves. They have not completely traded one model for another, but some have attempted to blend the contradictory messages about what it means to be a man into some kind of meaningful job description applicable today. The challenge for modern fathers is to find ways to transcend their fathers' legacies while choosing to keep the best of those legacies as well.

One professional economist described his dilemma this way: "I know that the traditional image of masculinity that I carry around comes from my father. He taught me that men provide for their families and don't show feeling. He was very traditional in this way, but he isn't a macho type—swaggering and tough-acting. He was just competent and reserved. Although I want to be able to show more feeling than he does, I haven't really repudiated all of him. I like his sense of competence, and it's important to me to still be like him in some ways" (*ibid.*, p. 12).

"Nurturing fathers" has become a catchphrase during the past few decades. More and more men are learning to feel and express their emotions. Scripture describes the most masculine Man who ever lived as a man moved by compassion and honest with His emotions. Jesus shed tears and did not feel less than a man. Jesus was reviled, but He didn't lash back. Unlike men today, Jesus controlled the one emotion that modern men are most likely to express—anger. The mark of Jesus is tenderness, a trait that many men consider less than masculine. If we are to use Scripture as our guide, then real men should be tender, compassionate, and expressive toward their wives, their children, and their God.

Bonding with their children has become more important with many modern fathers than in the past. Traditional sex roles did not allow men truly to bond with a child. As a result, men missed out on the real joy of parenting. More and more men today are becoming actively involved in the work of child rearing. A small number of men have opted to be househusbands and fathers, devoting most of their time to the family. A larger portion of men today share the important responsibility of parenting. Unfortunately, even among the enlightened few, there is often more talk than action.

Many men were taught that it is not possible for a man to express his emotions or bond with young children. Psychological and sociological theories have long neglected fathers—assigning them very limited roles with infants and young children. While it is true that we are a long way from full male participation in parenting, at least we are now headed in the right direction. Two-career families seemed to provide the needed excuse for many men to become more active as a parent. The employed mother makes it easier for fathers to devote more time to the children and to enjoy the bonding that only shared time can bring. The old theory that father interacts with the children only after he returns from work is no longer valid, since both parents now return from work equally exhausted.

Nurturing fathers today are often disappointed and feel angry when they attempt to become more involved in raising their children. They soon discover that it is almost impossible to combine serious child care with serious work at home in their vocations or paying professions. Men often feel angry over the burden of child care and then feel guilty because of that anger.

"Your responsibility and your kids' constant demands make it hard to do anything else that you really want to do. If you've got two children whining at you, there's really no way you're going to get the other things done. All you are is frustrated. That makes you angry with the children, and either you explode or you get depressed. Or you realize all of a sudden that you shouldn't be angry, that you'd better just put the work off until later. Nothing goes with child care except puttering" (Astrachan, *How Men Feel*, p. 243).

Research indicates that fathers can be just as nurturing as mothers if given the opportunity by society and mothers. Yes, contrary to popular opinion, mothers may shut out the fathers' attempts to nurture. It is easy for employed mothers to crowd fathers out when both return home after work. The mothers' actions may result from guilt or from an attempt to compensate for leaving the child with substitute care during the day. Whatever the reason, mothers are often more reluctant than is society to allow fathers to play an active nurturing role in child care.

Spending time with their children allows fathers to help form their children's gender identity. Men often relate with more rough-housing, whereas women cuddle and coo. Both examples are beneficial to the child for gender identification. Fathers teach masculinity to their sons by nurturance, domi-

Society, government, corporations, institutions, church, friends, neighbors, and even family members resist the attempts of men to be nurturing fathers.

nance, and time spent together. They also help their daughters prepare for womanhood by giving them opportunities to relate to a safe male. One of the tragedies of child sexual abuse is the destruction of that trust and a distortion in future relationships. Unfortunately, there seems to be an unspoken alliance against nurturing fathers, whether they are the primary or equal parent. Society, government, corporations, institutions, church, friends, neighbors, and even family members resist the attempts of men to be nurturing fathers. As a result of concrete casting by culture, many people are uncomfortable with what they perceive as role reversal. Fathers get a low priority from government, businesses, and even churches, all of which view nurturing fathers as trying to usurp the traditional female role as mother.

The general populace seems embarrassed by men who take time out from their careers to be nurturing fathers. Relatives take a dim view of men who are not good providers. (By that they mean gainfully employed.) Few employers are willing to give men time off to see their child in a school play. Schools often make fathers feel unwelcome among the mothers on a school trip or parent-in-classroom program. Because of this, few men take advantage of paternity leaves offered by their employers. They fear that it will cripple or at least curtail their careers.

One industrial engineer quit his job to care for his children while his wife finished medical school. When he tried to return to his career, he met with extreme prejudice and preconceived ideas. "I'm black and blue from being fended off by personnel managers with 10-foot poles who don't know that changing diapers doesn't cause leprosy." After five months of active job-seeking, he was offered only one job—at half his old pay. Disgusted with the whole process, he eventually gave up and went back to full-time fathering. Society has not yet made child care a matter of priority for parents of both sexes.

Fathers for the Future

Future fathers should be dreamers—those who dream for their children. Unfortunately, without careful monitoring, these dreams can drive fathers deeper into self-imposed exile at work as they try to earn enough money to make the dreams a reality. If they strive too hard to fulfill a dream, they may pass on the same legacy to their sons, namely that men are judged by the hours they work and the money they make, not by the time they spend with their children and spouses.

They must encourage their children to dream and help them work toward fulfilling that desire, but fathers must learn to dream *with* their children and not *for* them. Father-dreamers spend

> **Fathers must learn to give unconditional, sacrificial, and redemptive love apart from experiencing the unique bonding of mother and child. Fathers must give something that cannot be bought—themselves!**

time listening to their children's dreams rather than creating them for the children.

Fathers should also be *givers* and understand that the role of seed-giver is as important as that of childbearing. This is difficult for many men, since they may not know the actual moment of conception, so the whole process becomes rather nebulous or unreal. Mothers, on the other hand, experience a finality when giving birth. They know exactly when they felt the first kick, when they gave birth, and when the child was weaned from their milk. Fathers do not have such clear signposts to guide their way down an unfamiliar path as parent.

Fathers must learn to give unconditional, sacrificial, and redemptive love apart from experiencing the unique bonding of mother and child. Fathers must give something that cannot be bought—themselves! Toys cannot replace father. Time is not measured in quality but in quantity. Without quantity there is no quality. One of the greatest insults to a child is to spend time with the child while your mind is focused on seemingly more important concerns.

Bill Butterworth tells about the time his son's sixth birthday was approaching. His son had mentioned that he wouldn't mind having a party, and as his son was usually very specific about the kind of presents he liked, Bill asked him what he could get him. He expected his son to give a well-rehearsed reply, such as "I'd like a baseball glove; you can find it at Toys R Us, aisle 6, below the batting helmets; or a Parcheesi board that is between Pac-Man and Payday in aisle 1." But his son's request was a bit different. He replied, "Dad, I'd like a ball to play with for my birthday."

"Great! What kind of ball would you like?"

"Oh, I don't know, either a football or a soccer ball."

"Well, which would you want more?"

"Wel-l-l-l," his son said and then hesitated, "if you have some time to play ball with me this year, I'd really like a football so we could throw it back and forth in the backyard. But if you're gonna be real busy this year, maybe you better just get me a soccer ball, because I can play soccer with the rest of the kids in the neighborhood."

"Fatherhood, like Godhood, is, after all, a giving of life, a giving in, a giving up, a donation, a surrender. You give your child a life to lead, . . . and you follow. You give life to your child and your child to life, and that act of giving creates the most intimate bond imaginable, . . . and it also creates an absolute otherness, for the gift is not a gift if it is not an irrevocable donation, a surrender, a sundering. You give with abandon, but do not abandon; the child is forever linked. The gift is by one possessed, but does not possess; the child, once lifed, is forever separate. The child is your very flesh and blood, incarnation, living apart and without you" (James E. Dittes, *The Male Predicament: On Being a Man Today*, p. 214).

Fathers should not become annoyed when their children ask impossible questions. Rather, they should be proud that their children think they know the answers.

Fathers should also be *teachers*. "The greatest mission for men today is not to correct what is wrong in adults, but to reach and teach what is right to children and youth" (Edwin Louis Cole, *On Becoming a Real Man*, p. 191).

Values are best taught and caught in the home. It's been said that a well-adjusted man is one who can enjoy the scenery even with the kids in the backseat. Without a father-teacher, teen men do not know what real manhood is all about. Fathers should not become annoyed when their children ask impossible questions. Rather, they should be proud that their children think they know the answers.

Father-teachers interpret life for children, whether seen on the television screen or read from a book or observed in the mall. One familiar mistake of father-teachers was revealed by an 8-year-old boy discussing father problems with his little friend. The boy grumbled, "First they teach you to talk, then they teach you to walk, and as soon as you do it, it's 'Sit down and shut up!'" Fathers should remember that not only do they interpret life for their children, but they also interpret God for them. Children learn about God through the words and example of the parents, especially the father.

Fathers should learn how to become *motivators* for their children. Scripture tells the bittersweet story of King David and his two sons. One son David disciplined—and motivated; the other son he gave free rein—and alienated. Adonijah rebelled as a young man, evidently because he had not been disciplined or corrected. "His father, King David, had never disciplined him at any time—not so much as by a single scolding" (1 Kings 1:6, TLB).

As Edwin Louis Cole has pointed out, "The quickest way to destroy a child [and weaken character] is to give a child anything he wants *(On Becoming a Real Man,* p. 193). On the other hand, "when Solomon was to inherit the throne of his father, David prepared for the transition by giving his wealth to Solomon to carry out the construction of the Temple" *(ibid.).* However, David also admonished Solomon that he should seek wisdom before accepting the responsibility. David's admonition "became the basis for [Solomon's] requesting wisdom from God" *(ibid.).* A tale of two sons: Adonijah was spoiled, and he rebelled; Solomon was admonished, and he submitted. Loving discipline is a motivator for success, whereas lack of discipline often fosters failure.

The sheriff's office in a Texas city once distributed a list of rules titled *How to Raise a Juvenile Delinquent in Your Own Family*. The list included the following:

> **"You'll never beat out of your child what is wrong in your own life."**

• Begin from infancy to give the child everything he or she wants. This will ensure your child's believing that the world owes him or her a living.

• Pick up everything the child leaves lying around. This will teach him or her that responsibility can always be thrown off on others.

• Take the child's side against neighbors, teachers, police. They are all prejudiced against your child. He or she is a *free spirit* and never wrong.

• Finally, prepare yourself for a life of grief. You're going to have it!

Scripture admonishes, "Fathers, do not provoke your children to anger, but bring them up in the discipline and instruction of the Lord" (Eph. 6:4, RSV).

Sometimes that seems difficult to accomplish. One child had been a real pain in the neck all day. When supper finally came, Dad made him eat at a folding table in the corner all by himself. When it came time for grace, the father asked the boy to return thanks. Folding his hands and bowing his head, the little lad prayed, "I thank You, Jesus, that You have prepared this table before me in the presence of my enemies."

One speaker commented, "You'll never beat out of your child what is wrong in your own life." When a father sees his child doing something of which he disapproves, he might begin the correcting process by examining his own behavior. The book *Twenty-one Stayed*, written by Virginia Pasley, tells the story of 21 American soldiers who defected and stayed with the Communists during the Korean conflict. The author states that her research revealed that 19 of the 21 felt unloved or unwanted by their fathers.

The definition of *father* is really "family house." It is the father's responsibility to provide intimacy, discipline, love, and worth. Failure of the "family house" provides opportunity for cults and gang cultures. It is not coincidental that the most successful rehabilitation centers for delinquent teens are those that most closely approximate family life in a family house. Fathers must make their children feel as though they belong to the family and are an important part of their everyday experience. It is not the father's responsibility to make his children's decisions for them, but rather to let them see him make his.

"Fatherhood is the act of losing one's life and finding it, all at once. . . . It is an excruciating blend of intense investment, all-out surrender and commitment, and helpless sidelining, watching from the curb while the parade passes by. . . . Fatherhood—perhaps manhood—is like Godhood: standing by, in the margins, straining with eager longing for your creation to be complete but knowing that completion is possible only if you withhold the power to enact it. You want so hard to shape, but know that your shaping will sabotage the creation's capacity to shape itself and therefore subvert its fulfillment. . . . To be a father, to be God, to be a man, is to give your all to your creation, all your energy, all your manhood, all your power, put everything to work to make the creation successful—and then, when it's time, to give still more by surrendering all and letting go" (Dittes, p. 215).

Jesus provided a working model for fathers in one succinct sentence: "For whoever would save his life will lose it, and whoever loses his life for my sake will find it" (Matt. 16:25, RSV).

CHAPTER 8

"Hey, Buddy, Can You Bear Some Change?"

I (Marvin) needed a change. Pressures had built up inside me from trying to initiate what I thought were needed and worthwhile changes in my local workplace. Some friends and colleagues favored those changes, and some did not. Sounds pretty normal, doesn't it? But the pressure seemed to be hitting me particularly hard at this time in my life. I wasn't dealing with it as easily as I had in the past. Was I burning out? Was I going through a midlife crisis? Even after talking to a trusted colleague, I wasn't sure. All I really knew was that I felt boxed in and that I needed a change in my work.

Eventually I had an opportunity to try a whole new area of concentration, and I was excited. I mean, I was *really* excited. Finally the day came to begin my new responsibilities. I left home on a two-hour drive to my new job, my new office, and my new secretary. I was singing. About 60 miles down the road a slight uneasiness began to surface inside me, and I stopped singing and began pondering. The more I thought, the more questions came to my mind. I began to realize that this was indeed a new challenge. It was so new, in fact, that I didn't know how to begin what I was going to do. Then I stopped pondering and began doubting. I doubted whether I was capable. I doubted whether I was ready. I doubted whether I had made the right decision. I wanted my mommy! Well, maybe not Mom, but I did wish I were back in my old office with my good friend, who served as my associate and my secretary and who also was my wife.

By the time I pulled into the parking lot of the new office building, I was actually somewhere between nervous and petrified. I walked in, said good morning to the receptionist, and disappeared down the hallway. It looked pretty dark down the hall, but to my relief there was light in the adjoining office of a friend who had made a similar change about a year earlier. I slipped into his room and received encouragement from him for an hour before I went down to my new office.

I needed a change. Yes, I think I did. But what surprised me most was the power of the stressors as a result of my change. So much was new. But wasn't that what I wanted? Yes, but did all the new stuff have to be so . . . new? I felt out of control, and I didn't like that feeling. I didn't like admitting that I was frightened and unsure of myself.

Men often like to change things, but they want to be in control of those changes. As I look back on my life, I see that a great deal of it has been out of control and that the only way I have ever been able to make positive changes was to recognize reality and seek help. Seeking help is especially difficult for me, as it is for most men.

By the ripe old age of 24 my life had deteriorated into a pretty ugly mess. I had already gone through a failed marriage. I couldn't hold a steady job. I had an out-of-control alcohol problem, which was the root cause of the other two circumstances. My father was a recovering alcoholic, and you'd think I would have known better, but growth usually comes from personal experience and personal change. Growth is never inherited. Through Alcoholics Anonymous I recognized and admitted that I was powerless to control my problem. I renewed a long-suppressed desire to turn my life over to a "Higher Power." Even though I had grown up attending church, it was through this group that I learned the prayer that I now offer many times each day.

Serenity Prayer
"God grant me the serenity to accept the things I cannot change,
The courage to change the things I can,
And the wisdom to know the difference."

What a wonderful prayer and important guiding principle regarding change in one's life! To accept serenely that some things are beyond my power to control or change, to be courageous enough to tackle the areas in which I can effect change, and to be wise and honest enough to know and admit the difference.

Now, what about change in *your* life? Well, you're not really experiencing any changes right now? Wrong! Change is always going on to some degree. Some aspects of change have been or will be covered in other chapters regarding aging, spiritual growth, and relationships. These are areas of change that we often fail to recognize because they are more subtle. It's rather like the daily growth in your own children compared to the leaps in growth of your nephews and nieces whom you see only on occasion. Or, worse yet, it's like going to your 30-year high school reunion and discovering how everyone else has gotten so old-looking. Sudden changes often catch us off guard, but they are recognizable and usually elicit immediate action. Subtle changes, like aging, may occur without our knowledge until we look at an old photo album. Suddenly we become aware of what has been happening to us for years. Aging occurs slowly, and coping with it requires a more methodical approach.

Our basic response to change, when recognized or acknowledged, whether it is sudden or subtle, involves a series of personal questions.

What's going on?—Something has gotten your attention. You have felt or perceived some effect of change. What caused it? Try to identify the real root of the change. Is it something that just happened, or has it been building over a period of time? Do you want it to continue, speed up, slow down, or stop? Is it coming from outside, or did you do it to yourself?

> *Sudden changes often catch us off guard, but they are recognizable and usually elicit immediate action. Subtle changes, like aging, may occur without our knowledge until we look at an old photo album.*

What are my options?—Remember, there are always options. Take the time to actually write them out. Then talk them out with a trusted friend. A trusted friend or counselor can help you examine your choices more objectively.

Harry Cordellos was diagnosed at an early age with a severe eyesight problem that would gradually get worse and

> **There are always options. Take the time to actually write them out. Then talk them out with a trusted friend.**

result in blindness. He was never given adequate preparation for his final condition, and he became very depressed as a teenager. Unable to do many things that other young people did, Harry considered suicide to be his best option. He didn't know how or when, but someday the opportunity would present itself and he'd be ready. Then one day he was with a group of friends at a picnic. As usual, Harry was on the fringes—just sitting, listening, and talking to the occasional friend who would stop awhile to chat. He could hear the sounds of energetic teens and the boat that took skiers around the lake.

One of the adults came by and asked Harry if he would like to ride in the boat. At first he thought he shouldn't, because his parents had always discouraged him from normal activities, but finally Harry was persuaded. He found the boat ride to be exciting. The bouncing on the water and the spray from the boat were things he had not known before. Then someone had a brainstorm. "Harry, get in the water." They explained how they would put on his skis, place the rope just right, and give the signal when it was time to "hit it." Harry protested strongly at this insanity, but finally thought, *Hey, maybe this is the time to end it all anyway.* So into the water he went. How many times Harry fell is not known, but "blind luck" was not a figure of speech used that day. Finally Harry made a circuit of the lake.

From that moment a new light was shining in Harry's mind. He knew that he could do anything he really wanted to do, and he has spent the rest of his life demonstrating that. He learned how to operate a PBX switchboard and got a good job. He developed skills in skydiving, golf, skiing, and photography (yes, photography). I first became aware of Harry through the film *Survival Run*, produced by Pyramid Film and Video in Santa Monica, California. It shows Harry running in the Dipsea Run, a seven-mile race over some of the roughest terrain imaginable. He runs on the arm of a sighted friend, but you have to see it to believe it. I met Harry at the Boston Marathon, and I have the utmost admiration for him. He knows something about change and something about options.

When dealing with change, don't limit yourself with traditional thinking. You may need a unique and creative solution. When you're looking at your options, don't be afraid to look beyond the obvious. Let me illustrate.

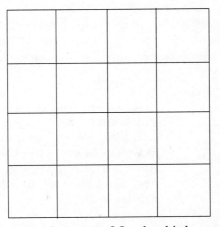

How many squares do you see? Look a bit longer, and you may increase your answer. Now, let me help you. First of all, there are the obvious 16 squares. Then there are nine more squares made up of four smaller ones. Now look for the four squares made up of nine, and finally the one made up of all 16. The answer, then, for the literalist is 30 squares. The real answer, however, is infinity. In addition to the 30 obvious squares, there are an infinite number of possibilities if one is not limited by the lines already drawn. Is that deceptive? Actually, that's not nearly as deceptive as the boxes of traditional thinking. It is important to explore one's possibilities and look beyond the lines already drawn by society or culture.

Where do I begin?—The good news is that if you've gotten to this question you have not only begun, but you're well on your way. You may also notice that something wonderful has now happened. First, you recognized and acknowledged that change was taking place and affecting you. Then, you considered your options, and now you're ready to take your first step in reaction. The difference is that something was happening to you, and now you are ready to make something happen. The wonderful thing is that you can always regain control. You may not always be able to stop the changing process, but you certainly can change how you relate to it. That puts you in charge again, and you'll feel better immediately. After I had stopped drinking and smoking, I thought that I was really on top of things and in control. About seven years later we moved overseas, where I worked at a hospital. As I was walking through the building one day, I spotted one of those scales that you stand on and slide the weights across the bar. You know, one of those brutally accurate ones. Well, I stepped up and put the big weight on

> *The wonderful thing is that you can always regain control. You may not always be able to stop the changing process, but you certainly can change how you relate to it.*

150 and started moving the little one over. I thought maybe it ought to balance at around 40, but it didn't. Ever so slowly I kept sliding it over, and to my dismay the crazy thing wouldn't balance even at 50.

Well, there was nothing else I could do if I wanted to know the truth, which I really didn't. I had to go find another scales, right? Unfortunately, it told me the same thing. The awful reality was that I weighed 208 pounds. At six feet tall and age 33 that was not good news. You know what I did? I called a friend and went with him to an AA meeting. There I found the courage to face the truth once again. I was not in control. I was not in charge. Soon after, I began an exercise regimen combined with a food monitoring program that consisted of simply evaluating the kinds of food I ate and the times at which I ate. After just six months I had lost 55 pounds.

How am I doing?—We all need to have someone who will be honest and tell us if we aren't moving fast enough, moving too fast, or if we are just kidding ourselves. I received my greatest help from Alcoholics Anonymous, a group of people who accepted me no matter what I did, but they would not allow me to be dishonest with myself.

This is the same type of relationship that we can all have with God, acceptance with a total honesty that loves too much to allow us to continue deceiving ourselves.

How far do I take it?—The key word here is "balance." How far is too far? What does God see as my potential? One problem that I will always have to face is that I have an addictive personality. It's very easy for me to go overboard on anything. I'm an alcoholic, recovering with 21 years of sobriety, thank you very much, but an alcoholic nonetheless. I'm also a former two-pack-a-day smoker. And I'm a former fatty. When I quit drinking, I did it all at once and forever. When I quit smoking, I threw the cigarettes away and never smoked again. When I decided to shed my fat, I did it with the determination that I'd get rid of all of it. My original goal was 165. When I reached it I thought I had better go some further to make sure I maintained it. I saw 160 and then 155. As I approached 150 I began thinking that 145 would be better, but my wife cautioned, "You're doing it again." I listened.

Running became very important to me. I enjoyed it. It was fulfilling. I was able to build up my endurance to 40 miles per week. I entered a few warm-up races and eventually ran my first marathon. Of course I had to better my time, and more intensive training quickly paid off. Soon I was averaging 70 miles per week. I enjoyed some real success with running and was even sponsored by Brooks. I entered and won some ultra-marathons, including 24-hour races in which I covered as many as 114 miles in one day. During several intensive training weeks, I exceeded 100 miles. It was taking a lot of my time, not to mention energy. I was doing it again. An addictive personality tends to do everything to excess, especially enjoyable things. It's amazing that my wife and I have only three children!

Obviously one is capable of becoming imbalanced by taking change and reform too far. Fortunately, I have a few proven friends (my wife being number one), who know me well and can keep me in check. On the other hand, many men are unable or unwilling to envision the full life that God desires for them. Consider the following series of lifestyle spectra on a scale of one to five.

1   2   3   4   5

Physical
1 = Dead. That's about the worst you can be physically.
3 = Absence of disease. This is what most people consider good health. The doctor says, "I can't find anything wrong with you," and we skip out with the news that all our tests were within the "normal" limits. The problem with that is that today the normal person dies of heart disease or stroke or cancer or something else delayable.
5 = Perfectly alive. This is intended to be the ideal. Because of our sinful human bodies, no one can be a 5.

If you're at 2, somewhere between dead and normal, then 3 might be an initial goal for you. After attaining your initial goal, set your aim a little higher, such as four. Later you might aim at 4.5; then 4.51; and then all the infinite other possibilities on your way to the ideal. Most people don't even recognize that anything above a 3 even exists. Many rely too much on medications to stay away from

1 and get to 3, when we should be exercising options, self-control, and our bodies to aim, at least, at 5.

Emotional

1 = Suicidal.

3 = Coping. Hanging in there. Getting by.

5 = You could explode because you're so happy!

Again, if you're a 2, then an initial goal of coping (3) is an appropriate beginning. But there's more to life than just coping. There's a great deal of life to explore once coping is no longer a problem. Everything up to a full 5 is yours for the seeking. Once again many men are using too much in the way of medication to reach the midpoint. Tranquilizers have their place, but they're not the solution. Men need to use change to their advantage, see their options more clearly, and stop to count their blessings in order to move beyond a 3. Helping others who are below us on this life scale will raise our emotional standing as well.

Social

1 = An incurable, unreachable hermit.

3 = One who tolerates others.

5 = Mr. Wonderful, who is literally everybody's best friend.

To move from 1 to 3 many use blockers such as alcohol or phoniness to "play the game." The game continues as long as it has some personal benefit. What men need is to move beyond toleration and aim at developing intimacy.

Most men have a real problem with

The truth is, there is far too much sex without intimacy and far too little intimacy apart from sex.

that last word because they associate intimacy with a sexual relationship. The truth is, there is far too much sex without intimacy and far too little intimacy apart from sex. Men are just beginning to scratch the surface of developing intimate relationships. A truly intimate relationship is usually safest and best between two men rather than between a man and a woman. For most men this removes sex from the picture. The problem with an otherwise intimate relationship between a man and a woman is that both are culturally conditioned to view sex and intimacy as two sides of the same coin. A man can certainly have an intimate relationship with his wife—and he should—but he also needs a male counterpart simply because there are some things about him that only another man can fully understand. To keep one's social and emotional balance, most men need a spouse and one or two intimate male friends with whom they can discuss anything and whose opinions they value and trust.

Spiritual

1 = Spiritually comatose (perhaps an atheist, although I've known atheists who still had a spiritual dimension).
3 = The pew warmer.
5 = A literal saint.

This is the most difficult one to work with because a 3 is really no better off than a 1. Jesus warned: "I wish that you were cold or hot, but not lukewarm" (see Rev. 3:15, NIV).

Perhaps a better definition would be this.

1 = Spiritually comatose.
2 = A pew warmer.
3 = Born again.
5 = A literal saint.

Three is certainly a giant step from 1 or 2, but it is only the beginning. Men can and should continue to grow toward 5 throughout eternity. We all need to be willing to let God change us so that we can continue to grow. The really good news is that God counts us as a 5 even though we might still be a 3!

Don't be afraid of change. Not only is it inevitable, but it's the most wonderful prospect I know. Remember, you are in charge! If you can't change your circumstances, you can always alter your attitude and reactions.

The changes I have observed in my own father throughout the years have been amazing. Because of his earlier alcohol consumption, he had to take an early medical retirement at age 55. He had been an auto mechanic all his life. I thought that repairing cars was all he could do. I really underestimated him. He developed a skill at and love for woodworking. When woodworking became physically uncomfortable, because of his health, he took up computers. Computers! My dad? Well, at 75 years of age he now types more than 50 words per minute and has a knowledge of and competence with computers that would land him a job in almost any office if it weren't for his age.

At 74 he got wide TV coverage in Seattle when he took a free bungee jump (awarded for being the oldest customer) from a 140-foot tower.

Change? Options? They are there for everyone. But change and options require each man to overcome his fear of jumping without a net.

CHAPTER 9

►◄

You're Only as Old
as You Feel
(Scary, Isn't It?)

I (Marvin) remember when I turned 10. I was proud that my age had two figures in it. As I walked to school that year (yes, back in those days we walked to school in the rain . . . and the snow . . . and it was uphill both ways) I often thought about how neat it was to finally be two digits old. Now as I approach three digits it has somehow lost its enchantment! The year after I reached two digits my dad turned 40. Now, that was old! He looked old. But then, my dad had always looked old. I looked at a picture of him recently that was taken when he was about that age. I guess the cameras weren't very good back in the old days, because he doesn't look nearly as old in the picture as I remember.

The problem is really one of perspective. You see, I've always been young. I was born at a very early age, and things really haven't changed in my mind all that much. When I went to the garage where my dad worked, all the other "old" men teased me and called me "kid." At my first several jobs I was always the youngest one there. I'm not sure when things began to change, but I do remember being shocked when a friend of mine, a few years younger than I, was asked to be a conference president. What was going on? They don't ask kids to be conference presidents. That's right, so guess what that means. Well, the truth is that I have a 2-year-old granddaughter. But at 47 I'm still a pretty young grandpa, wouldn't you say?

The good news, they say, is you're only as old as you feel. Well, that's good news only as long as *you* feel good. I've had a few days lately when how I *felt* would have made me eligible for receiving congratulations from Willard Scott.

We joke about aging a great deal, and a lot of the jokes are funny. It's good to be able to laugh at ourselves at times. But it's not always funny when I really have to face the fact that I can't do what I used to do or that I now have to do things that I didn't used to do. You might not fully appreciate all of this if you are still under 40, but trust me, you'll understand soon enough. So, what is this thing called aging, and how can I handle it gracefully?

Who wants to handle it gracefully? Never mind that old people are worth a fortune, with silver in their hair, gold in their teeth, stones in their kidneys, lead in their behinds, and gas in their stomachs!

> *I think the thing that hits men the hardest and tends to undermine self-worth the most is loss of physical performance. Obviously each man is going to be different, but sooner or later every man is going to be surprised and disappointed to realize that his body can't quite do what it did in his 20s.*

I think the thing that hits men the hardest and tends to undermine self-worth the most is loss of physical performance. Obviously each man is going to be different, but sooner or later every man is going to be surprised and disappointed to realize that his body can't quite do what it did in his 20s. The penny might drop on the basketball court, or while landscaping the yard, or in bed, but the day will come. Unfortunately, once you begin to recognize the truth, your body reminds you of the fact repeatedly. So, men, what are our options?

Remember the serenity prayer? Accept the fact that there are some things about aging that you simply cannot change. Your body is not going to last forever. But the second part of that same prayer asks for the courage to change the things you can. What are some of the things you can change that will tend to increase your longevity the most?

1. If you smoke, stop!—There is no single change you can make that will benefit your health and lengthen your life more than this. I know it can be a real challenge. I'm a former two-pack-a-day man myself, but you can do it, and there are plenty of individuals and groups around to help. If nothing else, you can contact me. I can help you quit.

It does take determination to make lifestyle

Alcohol is a depressant. It thickens the blood. It is calorie-laden. It is addictive.

changes, though, and I've seen some wonderful efforts. When I was working in Hong Kong I held many stop-smoking programs. One of the things we stressed the first night was that the participants needed to drink plenty of water. We suggested six to eight glasses per day. During one particular class when we assembled for the second night's session, I noticed that one Chinese lady seemed distressed. She sat for a while and then went out, coming back after a few minutes. Often people will feel a little ill during the time they are going through withdrawal, so I was not unduly concerned, but she left the room four or five times. Later in the evening we had a time for each one to share how his or her day had gone, and eventually this woman's turn came.

Almost in tears, she confessed that she had tried her best to follow the program faithfully, but alas, she had been able to drink only 32 glasses of water, far short of the 68 recommended!

With that she sloshed out the door once more.

2. Don't drink alcohol, or if you must, drink moderately.—As you might expect, I adhere to and promote the first option. There is no question in my mind that from a biblical perspective we should not use alcohol at all. There are too many other better choices for every situation where we do see it being used in Scripture. From a longevity point of view only, we must at least cut it down to a very moderate level of consumption. Alcohol is a depressant. It thickens the blood. It is calorie-laden. It is addictive. If you have to argue to defend its benefits, you may indeed have a drinking problem.

3. *Begin a regular exercise program.*—This is the third most important change you can initiate to increase longevity. In all these changes, more important than increasing quantity of years is increasing in *quality* of years. An exercise program is essential to well-being. Your physical, mental, social, and spiritual dimensions depend on it. Thirty minutes a day every other day is all it takes to assure improved quality of life.

If you succeed in really making this a regular lifestyle, expect that some people may try to undermine your efforts. Sometimes they are well meaning, but often they are jealous. In other cases they just don't understand.

Consider the following conversation between Hilda and Hans.

"Uff-da, Hans! Golfing is not gud for da heart," remarked Hilda.

"Vat makes yew say dat?" asked Hans.

"Vell," replied Hilda, "I yust heard a golfer say dat he had four strokes on da very first hole!"

4. *Get adequate rest.*—Seven to eight hours of sleep a night is still the magic number for the vast majority of us. Those hours before midnight are still better than the ones after midnight, too. Turn off the TV a little earlier. Take a 30-minute walk with your wife, your child, or a friend before retiring, and you'll find that you sleep better and awaken more refreshed. Try it!

> **The key to getting ahead in life is to set aside eight hours a day for sleep and eight hours a day for work. Unfortunately, I know too many people who are using the same eight hours for both!**

It has been said that the key to getting ahead in life is to set aside eight hours a day for sleep and eight hours a day for work. Unfortunately, I know too many people who are using the same

FCM-5

eight hours for both!

5. *Maintain proper weight.*—Be careful of the old Metropolitan Life weight tables. More recent studies have found that as we get older our bodies will naturally carry a little more weight without negative results. Balance and honesty are important here. If you need to shed a few pounds, then do it.

> **Don't make lifestyle changes a pain in the neck (or anywhere else for that matter). Just simplify your life a little, and you could reap big results.**

A moderate exercise program, combined with a few simple dietary choices, will work wonders.

Especially as we age we know how difficult this step can be. Keep your emphasis on the right place. Remember the point from this little exercise you can try on your friends. Have them pick a number between 1 and 10. Now double that number, add 6, divide by 2, and subtract the original number from the total. The number you are left with is 3.

Some will be able to do this in their heads, and some will need paper and pencil. Others will need someone else to figure it for them. The point of this exercise is not the answer, but rather the process. You already know the answer before you start.

The important thing in weight control, or in any other lifestyle change for that matter, is not the answer or the desired goal but rather the process. Take one day at a time and do each step as it comes, and the answer will take care of itself.

6. *Start the day right with a reasonable breakfast.*—It doesn't have to be fancy or heavy or time-consuming. Try some good fruit and some multigrain bread or cereal. Give your body some energy to begin the day's work on. This will also make number 7 a whole lot easier.

7. *Don't eat between meals.*—I know, I don't like to see this one

on the list either, but in a 20-year study done on lifestyle habits most effective for longevity this ranked number 7.

Maybe you just need to rearrange the furniture. You know, put the TV and the refrigerator farther apart. For too many people that walk is all the exercise they get.

The principle here, I believe, is simplicity. Don't make lifestyle changes a pain in the neck (or anywhere else for that matter). Just simplify your life a little, and you could reap big results.

To be sure, there are changes you can make to help you get the most out of what you've got. But you still have to deal with reality. No matter what you've got, it isn't going to last forever. I think, however, that we can learn to appreciate the changes that come in the later chapters of our lives.

In high school I ran on the cross-country and track teams. Competition was everything. I did fairly well, winning my share of races, and as a sophomore I got my mile time down to 4:42. During my junior year I only equaled that time, and in my senior year I dropped out to pursue other activities, like drinking, smoking, and girls. When, at the age of 33, I determined to resume running as a means of regaining fitness, I still was very competitive. I was running longer races now, but I still wanted to beat that old high school time. The closest I ever came was a 4:58 at age 35. Even though I focused on marathons, the principle was still the same. I always had to run a faster time. That works for a while, but somewhere along the way you run your fastest time. Unless you either quit or learn to run for reasons other than competition, you're going to have a tough time adjusting to your body's refusal to run that fast again. I'm happy to say that finally I have come to the place where I run simply because I love to do it. I still run races, but my enjoyment is in the fact that I can still be out there. I enjoy the people more. Participation is more important than performance.

We all need to be less goal-driven and focus a little more on enjoyment of life. Of course, we can go to extremes on that path, but most often we have gone to extremes on busyness. Achieving and having the answers are not what it is all about. The process is what's important.

The same thing is true in other aspects of life as well, including career and even sexual fulfillment. Sex may become less frequent as we age, but it can certainly get better. That is true only if you are developing a growing intimacy with your wife.

The problem too often is that our marriages are like a bathtub of hot water. Once you're in it for a while, it's not so hot.

One great way to keep your sexual relationship alive is to find good books on the subject—done in a way that appeals to both of you—and read them together. This opens up for you areas of discussion that may be difficult to enter into on your own. Keep learning and keep growing, and you'll keep your love life alive.

I love to see people who have learned to accept the things they cannot change and live life with zest. My father has enjoyed many things in the past that he has had to set aside, but he always finds something else to fill the vacuum, and he puts his whole heart into it. I guess that attitude runs in our family. My dad's aunt died at the age of 102. I still remember her father, who died at the age of 103, when I was about 6.

But Aunt Minnie was a special case. She outlived four husbands and was very outspoken about life. At 90 plus years she had a knee fused, and she began to do poorly while recovering in the hospital. The doctors said that she was just too old to recover, but she had other ideas. She refused to take any more medication, and two days later she checked out of the hospital, completely against her doctor's advice. I remember watching her, two years later, as she recarpeted her house. It was inspiring to see her stretch the carpet with a knee kicker by

> *Achieving and having the answers are not what it is all about. The process is what's important.*

getting into a three point stance and banging away with her good knee. At 94 her third husband passed away, and the gentleman from across the street, whose wife had recently died, began to visit. This went on for some months until finally he put his thoughts into words. "Minnie," he said, "at my age it's kind of dangerous to be crossing the road every day like this. I could get hit by a car. Don't you think it would be better if we both lived on the same side of the street?" The funny part of that was that they were the last two houses on a dead-end street. But they decided to marry, and when the minister asked if she would take him to be her lawfully wedded husband, she said, "I do, I do, I do!" We sort of expected birth announcements, but they never came!

Lifestyle habits, including exercise and diet control, are vital to optimum aging. Attitude, serenity, and courage play an equal role. Another key element is maintaining a healthy sense of humor. In his well-known book *Anatomy of an Illness*, Norman Cousins wrote about his battle with a crippling and potentially life-threatening disease of the connective tissue. His reading and studies convinced him that disease could be caused or made worse by emotional tension such as anger, frustration, or resentment.

Cousins posed this question: "If negative emotions produce negative chemical changes in the body, wouldn't the positive emotions produce positive chemical changes? Is it possible that love, hope, faith, laughter, confidence, and the will to live have therapeutic value?" (pp. 34, 35). He intended to find out.

In addition to his medicinal treatment, which he limited to ascorbic acid (vitamin C), he spent two hours each day watching videos of *Candid Camera* as well as old Marx Brothers films. He supplemented his comedy viewing by reading humorous books. His physicians took sedimentation rate tests before and after his laughter sessions and found a constant and lasting improvement each time.

Attitude is vital. Having a meaningful purpose in life and a sense of humor may not guarantee a long life, but it will certainly enable you to get the most out of what you have.

I'll never forget the first time I applied this principle to my own life. It was back at that wonderful age I mentioned at the beginning of this chapter. I was 10. Somehow I had gotten the idea that my allowance would go further if I didn't pay for everything I wanted. So I began slipping a few candy bars into my pocket when no one was looking. I got away with it three or four times until one day as I was heading for the exit I heard a voice over the loudspeaker say, "Bob, check that young man going out the door." I should have run, but I froze in my tracks.

Bob made me empty my pockets, and he found the candy bars. He marched me through the back room, upstairs, and into the manager's office. To my surprise, I looked down upon the stocked shelves below and realized that the big mirror I had seen from the first floor was actually a window in the manager's office. Well, now I was in a mess! Somehow I had to avoid having them notify my parents. I had a healthy fear of my father's wrath. So when they asked me my name, I made something up. When they asked me where I lived, I told them I had taken the bus and hitchhiked out from Chicago. (This took place in Edmonds, Washington, just north of Seattle.) Why didn't they believe me? Lucky for me, I thought, they didn't recognize me already. My parents shopped for groceries there every week. Finally, they told me just to sit tight and they were going to bring in a friend of mine. I wondered who that could be. A few minutes later I heard footsteps on the stairs, and I turned around and saw the gun, holster, and bullets belonging to the chief of police, who lived only one block from our house. He didn't know me either, and I stuck to my story. Well, I got marched down the stairs, through the store, and into the backseat of a police car. Did you know there are no handles on the inside of the back doors? I looked!

Down to the station we went, and they gave me one more chance to cooperate, but I was not budging. The result was that I was given the opportunity of inspecting the inside of a cell. I can still remember the sound of that metal door closing, followed by a heavy wooden door. I spent the next four hours just waiting in a small cell with a bunk, a toilet, and a little window that I couldn't squeeze through. I was one scared kid, let me tell you! Then I heard the phone ring. Of course, I could hear only one side of the conversation, but it was enough. It went something like this. "Yes, could you describe your son to me? Well, we have a young man here. I think you might want to come down and take a look."

> **I hope I can maintain my ability to laugh down to the last moment of my life.**

This was not good. My thoughts began to race. I pretty well figured what was coming. I knew something about judgment day when you're part of the "wicked."

As I pictured my certain fate I began to repeat one phrase: "I will laugh again. I will laugh again. It might not be tonight. [Understatement!] It might not even be for a few days, but I will laugh again."

A few minutes later I heard my parents' voices out in the office. Then the wooden door was opened, and I looked at my dad through the bars. His comment was, "It's a good thing those bars are there!" The chief took my dad by the arm and suggested that they have a little talk first. I would laugh again, but not that day.

I hope I can maintain my ability to laugh down to the last moment of my life. Consider the example I read about recently. An elderly man was very ill and near death. He was surrounded by his family, and the end was obviously near, because his loved ones were watching him closely. Finally his daughter observed, "I don't see him breathing. I think he's gone."

"He can't be," replied her brother. "His feet are still warm. No one ever died with warm feet."

At this point the old man sat straight up in bed and exclaimed, "Joan of Arc did!" Immediately he lay back down and was gone.

Wouldn't it be great to go out with a superb one-liner as your final comment on life?

The real bottom line is simply to enjoy life. Take care of yourself, yes. Make some lifestyle changes, yes. Keep learning, yes. But enjoy the process. Men often grow old before their time simply because they don't stop to enjoy the process.

CHAPTER 10

Men-Who-Pause!

I (Len) stood alone in the Arizona desert. The stars cast a faint glow on the cactus and tumbleweed, allowing me to view their shapes in the night. My mind felt like a rock tumbler as thoughts and questions rolled around in my head. *Lord, what am I doing here? How could my life change so completely in one year? When is it all going to end? Will things ever get any better?*

Two years earlier, my life had been exciting, stimulating, and fulfilling. I seemed to be approaching some kind of peak in my career. Now my life was empty, depressing, and filled with anger. I had reached a new low. During the past year I had lost my father, my job, my health, and my relationship with God. Former friends were whispering to each other behind my back. Even my wife was beginning to wonder why I was so depressed. What more could I lose? My life? It might even be a relief. Everywhere I looked, my life seemed to be going rapidly downhill, and I felt out of control.

The key word in male midlife is *loss*. Gravity begins to have its inevitable victory over your body. Your stomach has prevented you from seeing your feet for a number of years. The hair on your head is more easily combed with a washcloth than with a brush. As Earl Wilson is quoted as saying, "Middle age is when your clothes no longer fit, and it's you who needs the alteration!"

Imagine the scene. You are at the beach and sitting in the shade of a large umbrella. You cannot help noticing the lean physiques of the younger men in their late teens and early 20s. What a difference between their abdominal concavity and your flabby, abominable convexity!

As you rise to your feet you self-consciously "suck up your guts"—like they taught you in the Army years ago. You're doing your best to put on a good "front." Looking down (trying to be casual, of course), you notice a slight outward bulge in your abdomen. You tighten your muscles even more and square your shoulders. However, when you start walking toward the water, you quickly realize that your unnatural gait resembles more that of an ape than an Olympic athlete. As you meditate on your physical condition you relax, and when next you survey your anatomy you observe that your ample waist is again hanging over your swimming trunks.

From that day on you begin to be very conscious of pulling in your stomach. Not infrequently you

Our bodies are fearfully and wonderfully made. They have marvelous restorative powers. But they have their limitations. So what is the midlife male to do?

catch your reflection in a mirror or a store window and—oops! your "chest" has slipped. You also remember the not-so-concealed looks of younger members of the human race as they observe your "pot" hanging over your belt. You try unobtrusively to slip into your Charles Atlas stance (only those who have reached middle age will remember him), but it's hopeless. So you continue on your way, hoping not too many people have noticed your momentary digression.

Our bodies are fearfully and wonderfully made. They have marvelous restorative powers. But they have their limitations. So what is the midlife male to do? His body is beginning to show visible signs of disrepair. Like an old building, the roof is in trouble, mortar is coming out of the joints, the floors are sagging, and the doors are beginning to creak. However, with the technology of the nineties, there is ample opportunity to restore your body to a fit condition. A good motto to live by is Think health, talk health, act health. Do that and you'll go a long way toward being healthy.

Your career is at a standstill. Your first decade was one of rapid upward movement, but the pace has slowed considerably in the past few years. The midlife male often feels impaled on the horns of a dilemma of his own devising. His obvious choices are either to stay put, writhing in agony in an occupation he dislikes, or push himself free and fall into the bottomless pit of that nothingness known as unemployment and failure.

Many women fail to understand fully the intense terror a man feels regarding his work. A man tries to come across as strong and secure. He wants everyone to think that he knows where he's going in life. To him, his job is an important part of his self-image, interwoven into the very fabric of his being. Stress produced by unhappiness with his work combined with the fear of losing his job (and consequently his self-worth) produces unbelievable extremes in his emotional life as well as maladies such as ulcers, high blood pressure, colitis, impotence, and nervous breakdown.

If the midlife male chooses to change occupations or is fired from his job, what then? Upon what depths of reserves does he draw when his whole world is already topsy-turvy? His unemployment could actually be a blessing in disguise, since he is free to try what he may have lacked the courage to attempt while still employed. It is also a time for him to become better acquainted with his own unique abilities through testing that is available at most universities and technical schools. Many men have picked themselves up from the devastation of midlife and successfully embarked upon another career.

George Foreman, onetime heavyweight boxing champion of the world, found himself defeated at the peak of his career by Muhammad Ali. Picking himself up from the canvas (to which he would return a decade later), he gave himself to Christian service. Albert Schweitzer, before the age of 40, had achieved international fame as one of the great interpreters of Bach. He had also written a book that ultimately became a theological classic among seminary students throughout the world. In addition, he was a very wealthy man. Yet Schweitzer did not feel fulfilled, so at the age of 38 he left it all behind and went to the interior of Equatorial Africa to serve as a missionary to those who could never pay for his services.

For your encouragement, Abraham Lincoln entered the Black Hawk War as a captain and came out a private. F. W. Woolworth got a job in a dry goods store when he was 21, but his supervisors wouldn't let him wait on any customers, because he "didn't have enough sense." Colonel Sanders of Kentucky Fried Chicken fame, after most men would have retired, became a millionaire by promoting a chicken recipe that he had been using in a little (going nowhere) roadside stand for years. The inventor of one of the most successful games ever created, Monopoly, was an unemployed worker in Atlantic City, New Jersey, during the Depression. George Burns expressed it this way: "Retirement at 65 is ridiculous. When I was 65 I still had pimples!"

Those who fail in midlife often do so because they are constantly thinking "sacrifice" rather than "possibility." By centering your attention upon achieving your goal, you make the obstacles seem smaller. By visualizing yourself as already attaining (and enjoying) your goal, you are more than halfway there. You need to turn your focus away from what you are giving up (like security, income, etc.) and think instead about what you will gain. When your attention is focused upon the end result, to the exclusion of all else, the desire to do anything that might delay its fulfillment is lessened considerably. As the Greek philosopher Epictetus once said: "It is not the event, but one's viewpoint toward the event that is important."

Men-who-pause begin to reexamine all those cherished beliefs and truths that have sustained them in the past. It's almost like going through a second adolescence, only this time they are too old to run away to the army and then sort out their confusion.

An emotional earthquake has shaken them inside, and they feel trapped beneath a rubble of responsibilities.

> **Those who fail in midlife often do so because they are constantly thinking "sacrifice" rather than "possibility."**

Surely there has to be more to life than constant pressure and demands from their employer, friends, and family. When they look into the future they see only decay, decline, and downward mobility. For some, their spiritual life is at its lowest ebb. To those whose lives have become spiritual vacuums, midlife can become an awesome shadow that chases away the dreams of youth and dashes the visions of the future.

Like the author of the biblical book of Ecclesiastes, some midlife males cry out: "All is vanity and a striving after wind" (Eccl. 1:14, RSV). Men-who-pause sometimes reject almost every belief that they have cherished from childhood and start over. Some will never be the same and will either discount religion entirely or, more likely, change churches or even denominations. Others will go through a "rebellious" period during which they question every church standard and doctrine. Eventually, they arrive at a revised set of standards, which they implement in their own lives. Still others will conclude that their spiritual lives need depth and commitment, and so they dedicate themselves to learning more about God and His plan for their lives.

Many midlife males feel unhappy or empty, yet they cannot seem to pinpoint the cause. They seem to be searching for meaning through something "out there." Actually, they are looking in the wrong place. Once their gaze settles on the cross of Jesus Christ, they find the answer to their uneasiness. Men-who-pause need Jesus! A total surrender to Christ enables them to rise above their problems and look at life more objectively. Once midlife males have found Jesus, they also discover value and worth in their own lives. An early Church Father, Augustine, summed it up with these words: "Our spirits are restless until they find their rest in God."

It was a confused midlife Pharisee who came to Jesus in the middle of the night to inquire about eternal assurance and its true source. "You must be born again!" Jesus replied. Sensing the inner turmoil that this midlife Pharisee was experiencing, Jesus explained to Nicodemus: "God so loved the world that he gave his only Son, that whoever believes in him should not perish but have eternal life. For God sent the Son into the world, not to condemn the world, but that the world might be saved through him" (John 3:16, 17, RSV).

It was this same unconditional love that prompted Jesus to ask an impulsive, uneducated, smelly, midlife fisherman named Peter to be His disciple. Peter—the aspiring water walker, the tempter who tried to prevent Jesus' Jerusalem mission, the ear-slashing hero who tried to redeem himself for falling asleep in Gethsemane, the dogmatic friend who

Jesus will pour out His unconditional love into your midlife madness until you too become a "new creation" in Him.

vehemently swore he didn't even know Christ, the ministry dropout who went back to his old ways as soon as Christ left the scene. Yet into this unpredictable, midlife male Jesus poured love, information, affirmation, rebuke, responsibility, assurance, and trust. As the lover and enabler, Jesus saw the potential in this midlife fisherman. You can read the results in the first 12 chapters of the book of Acts.

In a similar way, Jesus will pour out His unconditional love into your midlife madness until you too become a "new creation" in Him. It is important to remember that in order for midlife males to realize the dynamics of the gospel in their lives, they must become both vulnerable and affirmative to those with whom they live. There are risks involved. But men-who-pause need to take the risks involved in relationships. They need to live and love just as Jesus lived and loved.

God's Word will provide "soul food" to heal your wounds and restore your sense of self-worth. But no one can read that Word for you. No one can pray your prayers for you. Others may have you on their prayer list, but that cannot take your place before God. Search the Scriptures and begin to look for solutions to your problems. The Bible was written for people going through a midlife crisis. You may find it comforting to read the suffering, despair, blame, and final assurance presented by the songwriter in Psalm 102.

Search the Word of God. Look for experiences similar to your own, and you'll find solutions as well as salvation. In your search, you may find the answers that you are seeking, and in the process discover what is truly important in life.

Men-who-pause do so for many reasons. Some pause because they feel trapped by their marriage or family. Others may experience burnout on their job or in their career. Men often pause when they come face-to-face with their own mortality and become fearful of the future. Many pause to examine a general uneasiness that is difficult to describe. It's like standing on the edge of an emotional precipice. Men-who-pause sometimes become obsessed with their health and physical condition. The youthful myth of immortality now becomes a mission of denial. As Picasso once said, "It takes one a long time to become young."

It is a sad commentary on life that we seem to spend one fourth of our lives growing up and three fourths growing old. The midlife transition is intertwined with all of one's former (and future) life. Everything a person has done and thought in the past and everything he will do and think and become in the future is all a part of the midlife crisis. Yet the one fourth of our life spent growing up is seen as the ultimate age by many midlife males.

The present generation is caught up in the transition from a parent-oriented society to a youth-oriented one. Youth has become the key to current advertising and only adds fuel to the fire of insecurity already burning within the midlife male.

Have you noticed the trend in advertising? Teenagers always seem to have bright, glistening, and straight teeth, while adults have dentures and bad breath. The young wife makes a cup of coffee that turns her husband into a sex maniac, but the middle-aged wife spends all day washing, mopping, and ironing, only to have her husband come home tired and cross with aching muscles, hay fever, allergies, bunions, and a headache with Excedrin written all over it. Young people wear sneakers and sandals, have fun, and laugh even with their mouth full of hair, but older people wear support hose and girdles, have constipation, pyorrhea, tired blood, and insomnia. Someone once wrote, "Middle age is when anything new in the way you feel is most likely a symptom." If the current emphasis on youthfulness continues, the next generation may go through midlife crisis at 30!

Male midlife crisis is a relatively new phenomenon because of our increased life expectancy.

Male midlife crisis is a relatively new phenomenon because of our increased life expectancy. During the Bronze Age the average male lived only 18 years. At the height of the Greek civilization it rose to 20. During the Middle Ages the life expectancy was 31. During the nineteenth century in the United States, it was only 37. Now the average male approaches 80 during his lifetime. With more and more males living to experience midlife, the symptoms have become easier to recognize and define. Bob Hope defines middle age with his famous quip, "You know you've reached middle age when your weight lifting consists of standing up and your birthday candles cost more than the cake."

Somewhere between the ages of 35 and 50, approximately 80 percent of males will pause to experience some form of midlife crisis or transition. Most will question where they've been, what they believe, and wonder if they're merely loitering on the road of life. It may have dawned on them that a few of their classmates have already died from heart attacks and that their own parents are putting their affairs in order. The midlife male recognizes that he is next. He takes little comfort in Joseph Heller's reassuring comments, "I've come to look upon death the same way I look upon root-canal work. Everyone else seems to get through it all right, so it couldn't be too difficult for me."

Life is happening too fast. The midlife male has already experienced more than half of his life and finds that he feels helpless, trapped, and angry.

Looking back, he realizes that he has climbed the mountain without pausing to enjoy the view from the top. Now he is walking down the other side at a rapid pace. Soon he may be so far down the slope that he may never have an opportunity to enjoy the view, so he pauses! But the slope is slippery, and his footing is unsure. Frantically he looks around for something or someone to cling to. No! Not the same motivators or beliefs that encouraged him to climb the mountain. Something different. Something he hasn't experienced before. Something he missed in his frantic struggle to the top.

His eyes scan the mountainside, and he sees younger climbers on their way up. If he could only be like one of them again, he might make it back to the top. This time, he promises himself, he'll take time to enjoy the view.

His gaze swings back to those around him on the downward slope. They all look so old. What has happened to their bodies? Their hair? Why are they wearing such out-of-date clothing? Looking back up the mountain at the younger climbers, he determines to get in shape, buy a toupee, and go shopping at a clothing store specializing in younger men's styles. Perhaps if he looks like a young climber they'll let him "hook up" with them, and he'll be able to climb the mountain again.

Pausing to catch his breath, he realizes that he has become exhausted just trying to stay in place on the mountain. He feels someone pushing him to begin his downward

Somewhere between the ages of 35 and 50, approximately 80 percent of males will pause to experience some form of midlife crisis or transition.

journey again. Cautiously he looks back into the worried faces of his wife and children. "Why have you stopped?" they ask hesitantly. "Keep going down the mountain. It's easier that way." Feeling their unwelcome encouragement as unwanted pressure, he pushes them away and almost loses his footing in the process. Turning away from them, he focuses his gaze in another direction while clinging precariously to a scrub oak.

Frantically clinging to his fragile foothold on the downward slope, his thoughts are interrupted by a young woman passing nearby on her climb up the mountain. His eyes linger on her beauty, and his thoughts fabricate flights of fantasy. *Maybe she can help me climb back up the mountain,* he muses. Hesitantly he raises his hand to wave. Flattered at his attention, she returns his greeting. Encouraged, he beckons her to his side. Thankful for an experienced guide to lead her up the mountain, she joins him, and they touch. His body seems rejuvenated with youthful energy as she responds, "Yes! I would love to climb the mountain with you." Ignoring the pleas of his wife and children, he starts back up the mountain with his new climbing companion.

"Where are you going?" an inner voice asks.

"Where are you going?" an inner voice asks. Pausing, he wonders who has spoken. God? No. It must be his imagination. Besides, it was such a "still small voice." If God didn't want him to go back up the mountain, surely He would speak louder and more distinctly. Besides, it's God's fault that he's on this downward slope. He didn't ask to be placed on this mountain. Surely God wants him to have one last view from the top before he slips into oblivion. Determined, he grasps his new companion's hand tightly, and together they begin to climb again.

Not all men-who-pause go through each aspect of midlife. For some it is merely a pause to catch their breath, but for many it is an uncomfortable transition filled with fear and doubt. For a few, it is a terrible crisis from which they never fully recover. Like it or not, all midlife males will eventually move on to the next stage of life. Some accept it gracefully and move on with their family. Others pause until they find new companions for their journey. A few remain in midlife until death.

While I stood there in the desert, I realized that there was no turning back. I could not change events. I could only learn from them. God had not deserted me; I had turned away from Him. There in the darkness, God seemed to be reassuring me that men-who-pause can actually begin again, that it was OK for me to pause and catch my breath before continuing life's journey, but continue I must. My journey would not take me back up the mountain, but it would continue on the well-worn path down the mountain. I had a renewed sense of anticipation about what was ahead. A Bible text kept flashing into my mind like a caution light at a dangerous intersection: "I can do everything God asks me to with the help of Christ who gives me the strength and power" (Phil. 4:13, TLB).

The crisis was over. Life would go on. I had not sought another companion to help me climb back up the mountain. My wife held tightly to my hand and offered love and support. My son extended his hand in friendship and understanding. And God became more real in my life than ever before.

A few months later I found new employment and a new purpose in life. My health problems were cured. My grieving for my father became bearable. I have not looked back up the mountain since that night in the desert. Perhaps it's because I'm too busy enjoying the view on the way down.

Questions for Midlife

Answer no more than five questions at a time. Write your answers in a notebook and keep them for future reference. Review your answers every six months and note any changes.

• Have I been living for myself and in accordance with my God-given talents, or have I been trying to meet someone else's expectations?

• How flexible am I in adjusting to life's changes?

• Can I truly accept the realities of life and aging?

• Can I trust the other adults in my life to take care of themselves?

• Can I allow people to help me without feeling demeaned or less of a man?

• How well am I coping with the fact that my body doesn't look or feel as good as it once did?

• How do I take it when my friends change, divorce, or even die?

• How well will I be able to deal with the death of my parents?

• What do I need in a marriage partner?

• What would I gain if I threw it all away and started over? What would I lose? What relationships would be irreplaceable?

• What do I want to do with the rest of my life?

• Who is Jesus?

Survival Techniques for Midlife

• Don't just do something; stand there! Resist the urge to make life-changing decisions while in the pause mode. It is extremely dangerous to make major decisions when you are emotionally unstable. Many midlife males are tempted to trash their entire past and start anew. This seldom cures their real problems and often creates almost insurmountable problems for the future.

• Recognize that teaching mountain climbing can be just as rewarding as actually climbing the mountain. Become a mentor. Experience the joy of sharing your abilities and knowledge with a younger person. You will both find the relationship rewarding.

Can I allow people to help me without feeling demeaned or less of a man?

• Allow time for transition. Midlife is a process, not an event. It's about *who* you are, not *what* you are. Take time to listen to yourself and God's "still, small voice."

• Live in the present. Enjoy each moment as a precious gift from God. Take mini-vacations—from an hour to a full day—and get in touch with yourself and your environment. Remove yourself from the time warp that keeps you looking back at your young adult life. Begin to focus on what you like to do now! Gandhi once said, "There is more to life than increasing its speed."

• Break new ground. Learn new skills. Challenge yourself outside your comfort zone. Get out of your rut and experience a wider selection of life. Take some night classes. Start a new hobby. Follow former President Carter's example and devote time to helping the less fortunate, and develop new skills at the same time.

• Cultivate family relations. Reconnect with your children and spouse. Reunite with extended family. Long-distance telephone is relatively inexpensive with the right package. Use your phone to contact a different relative every month.

• Focus on your spiritual life. To find answers to the meaning of life, allow God to speak to you through His Word, private prayer time, and/or journaling (writing out your prayers to God). Challenge yourself to read the Bible slowly from cover-to-cover, and write down in a special notebook thoughts that come to you. Review and read from your notebook periodically.

• Anticipate the rest of life's journey. Look forward to each stage of life as an exciting new journey that you have not taken before. Imagine the shape of your ideal life one year from today, and then work backward to formulate a series of goals that will take you there. William Shakespeare once wrote, "We know what we are, but know not what we may be."

CHAPTER 11
▶◀

Provider, Protector, and Priest

A myth out there won't seem to go away: Man is the priest of the home and provides sustenance, protection, and leadership for his family. Some women perpetuate this myth while others challenge it, but most men try to adhere to it. Why? There are myriads of reasons. The fact remains, however, as we enter the twenty-first century that it is becoming increasingly more difficult for men to fulfill the roles of provider, protector, and priest.

Gary Larson in one of his *Far Side* cartoons showed a posse of men hanging on to the leash of a bloodhound that was faithfully and energetically doing what bloodhounds are supposed to do. The words in the little cloud coming out of the dog's mind said, "I can't smell a thing!" That speaks volumes, doesn't it?

As a man I envision all these people hanging on to follow my lead, and a great deal of the time I realize that I haven't a clue. I just keep plunging ahead, hoping that I'll pick up the scent again somewhere down the trail. I also desperately hope that those who keep hanging on won't realize that I'm lost. After all, I'm supposed to be the leader.

These are truly challenging times for men. The male role appears to be in a state of flux. With such uncertainty, how does one determine what the male role ought to be? Perhaps we need to start at the beginning.

"The Lord God formed the man from the dust of the ground and breathed into his nostrils the breath of life, and the man became a living being. . . . The Lord God said, 'It is not good for the man to be alone. I will make a helper suitable for him.' . . . So the Lord God caused the man to fall into a deep sleep; and while he was sleeping, he took one of the man's ribs and closed up the place with flesh. Then the Lord God made a woman from the rib he had taken out of the man, and he brought her to the man. The man said, 'This is now bone of my bones and flesh of my flesh; she shall be called woman, for she was taken out of man.' For this reason a man will leave his father and mother and be united to his wife, and they will become one flesh" (Gen. 2:7-24, NIV).

Apparently God originally intended equality of the sexes. But after sin became part of the

God originally intended equality of the sexes.

human predicament, God spoke to Eve, saying: "I will greatly increase your pains in childbearing; with pain you will give birth to children. Your desire will be for your husband, and he will rule over you" (Gen. 3:16, NIV).

From that time on, Scripture basically portrays a male-dominated society. To be sure, societies do not always operate all that well, but throughout biblical times men played the role of provider, protector, and priest of the family. Consider these often-quoted words of Paul to the church in Ephesus: "Wives, submit to your husbands as to the Lord. For the husband is the head of the wife as Christ is the head of the church, his body, of which he is the Savior. Now as the church submits to Christ, so also wives should submit to their husbands in everything" (Eph. 5:22-24, NIV).

Although many men stop reading at this point, Paul continues to elaborate about how husbands need to care for their wives as Christ cared for the church and was willing to give His life for her. The apostle was in no way implying a dictatorial, abusive relationship. Just the opposite! If men truly love their wives as Christ loves the church, their relationship will be one of respectful enabling and elevation to the highest plane.

However, it is still a relationship based on male leadership. Scripture presents a consistent portrayal of the male role, following Christ's example, as the provider, protector, and priest.

The world of the Bible was, indeed, a man's world. It was not ideal or God's original plan, but it was fact. Our society from that time to this has been, for the most part, a male-dominated world. Men have pretty much run things and wielded the power.

However, the male role today is not the same. Women are entering all kinds of arenas that previously were reserved for men only. One of the difficult admissions for many men is to acknowledge that women are doing a good job. What does all this mean to Mr. Macho Man as he enters another millennium? For many, it's a time of confusion, frustration, and uncertainty about their masculinity.

The question many men are asking is Why should my masculinity be in question just because the role of women in society is changing? But change has always been inevitable. Since most men base their masculinity on cultural expectations, now that our culture is changing they will have to accept a demasculinized role, become a male chauvinist pig, or rethink their definition of a man.

Provider—Throughout history, until very recently in our Western society, and in many primitive societies the man has been the primary (sometimes sole) provider for the family.

I grew up in the fifties and early sixties. I think I was about 10 when my mom went to work. As I recall, that really seemed strange to me. Almost all my friends' moms were at home.

My dad was an auto mechanic, and we appeared to live comfortably. (What does a 10-year-old know?) My parents, my older sister, and I lived in a one-bedroom house, but I didn't know any other way. My folks, however, realized that if my mother found a job outside the home, they could significantly upgrade their lifestyle. In just a few months we moved to a house with three bed-

Women are entering all kinds of arenas that previously were reserved for men only. One of the difficult admissions for many men is to acknowledge that women are doing a good job.

rooms. Wow, I had my own room!

I remember when payday came every week. My parents were quite open about their finances, and it just seemed normal that Dad's check was always bigger than Mom's. Mom didn't complain, and although Dad used to say that he wouldn't mind if she did make more money than he, I had this feeling that it would be wrong if she did. Dad was the provider. Mom was just helping out.

Today very few families live on a single income. The full-time homemaker, not employed outside the house, is the exception. In addition, more and more women are either sole providers for a one-parent family or are making more money than their husbands. Men are no longer the sole providers in the majority of modern families and increasingly are not even the primary providers.

By choice some husbands fulfill the role of "Mr. Mom" and are not employed outside the home at all. Although this is a valid choice and in most cases works very well, such men often take intense criticism, both verbal and nonverbal, from other men. The age that has demanded equal pay for equal work and has prohibited discrimination based on race, religion, sex, age, height, weight, etc., has brought with it the necessity to rethink some of the traditional male roles.

Most men would find it very difficult to provide satisfactorily for their families on just their incomes. Plus many women enjoy their work and don't want to give up their career choices after marriage. So if society modifies the male role as provider, what determines his masculinity?

Protector—Surely this is an area in which masculinity is defined, right? Picture the caveman valiantly defending his family from a saber-toothed tiger. Or what man has not pictured himself as John Wayne, rescuing the helpless young woman from the bad guys? After all, weapons were invented by a man to protect him and his family from unsavory characters.

Today there's a definite shortage of wild tigers. In fact, our enemies are sometimes difficult to identify. In today's legal system only a fool defends himself, because the law is so complicated that the aggressor often has more rights than the victim!

As if all this weren't bad enough, consider the humbling fact that more and more women are becoming extremely adept at self-defense and can often disable an attacker quicker than her protective male friend could.

Many women enjoy their work and don't want to give up their career choices after marriage. So if society modifies the male role as provider, what determines his masculinity?

I recently visited some friends who informed me that their daughter, an attractive young woman in her 30s, was taking self-defense classes.

"Let me show you," she offered quietly. Somehow, secretly, I was relieved that she directed the statement to her stepfather rather than to me. Lying on her back, she directed, "There, now you kneel down on top of me and pin me down."

With confidence good old stepdad, who seriously looks like he could play running back for the Chicago Bears, pinned the hapless, slender, 125-pound victim.

Suddenly there was a movement, and the attacker was semi-airborne, over her head, and headed toward the fireplace. Not only did she disable her attacker, but she did it while he was expecting it!

"Wasn't that fun?" she asked with a smile as she offered to let me have a try. Fortunately, I had a pressing engagement elsewhere. Another time, perhaps. . . . Not!

In today's urban society, women often carry whistles, stunblasters, mace, and a certificate, if not a black belt, in self-defense. And have you seen the number of kids in those classes and the way that they can throw full-size instructors around? Well, maybe the male role as protector is not as essential as it was in more primitive times. In fact, maybe the average male is no longer equipped to fulfill his role as protector.

Priest—As a boy growing up, I knew some pretty impressive Christian women. At the church I attended they even had women who were ministers, although none of them were in charge of a church. They were involved in some form of teaching ministry, or perhaps they had served as missionaries overseas. Real ministers were men. This conclusion was obvious from the male exclusivity among the biblical priesthood, the disciples and apostles, and the male dominance throughout all Scripture.

"And they [the four living creatures and the 24 elders around the throne] sang a new song: 'You are worthy to take the scroll and to open its seals, because you were slain, and with your blood you purchased men for God from every tribe and language and people and nation. You have made them to be a kingdom and priests to serve our God, and they will reign on the earth'" (Rev. 5:9, 10, NIV).

A multitude of Bible texts show—even from modern translations—that God's work was predominantly through men. When the present authors went to college, there were a few young women studying to become what our denomination called "Bible workers," but none seriously studied to be pastors. That was only 20 years ago. Today most denominations ordain women to the gospel ministry, and more and more women are pastoring churches. Many serve as senior pastors. Those organizations that are not yet ordaining women are currently debating the issue.

Women in ministry today are really doing a good job. They add a whole new approach and dimension to the task. They bring new creativity, compassion, and commitment. Some men (those who are hesitant to accept female pastors), I suspect, are intimidated, and perhaps they have reason to be. Many women are doing a better job of pastoring than men have, and few of them become sexually involved with their parishioners.

I have always thought it interesting that when the Pharisees asked Jesus to rebuke His disciples and keep them silent, His response was "I tell you, . . . if they keep quiet, the stones will cry out" (Luke 19:40, NIV). If Jesus would use rocks to accomplish His mission, surely He would not hesitate to use women. Yet some men today still struggle with the idea of women in ministry.

The real issue here is not whether the church ought to use women in ministry, but rather how we men are going to react to the fact that the church already has recognized women in pastoral roles.

Another thought to ponder: How can men exclusively claim the position of priest in the home when there are so many more women in church than men? Does that mean that in churches in which women outnumber men two to one each man should be priest in two homes? It just doesn't make a lot of sense, does it?

So where does all this leave a Christian man? If the modern Christian male acknowledges that his female counterpart may well be able to provide, protect, and give priestly direction—what is left for him?

One's security as a man is in serious question if it is rooted in traditional, stereotypical roles. The new male needs desperately to come to grips with God's role for him as a man, rather than culture's expectations.

God's Commission

"He has showed you, O man, what is good. And what does the Lord require of you? To act justly and to love mercy and to walk humbly with your God" (Micah 6:8, NIV).

This text is not speaking exclusively to the male sex any more than is the rest of the Bible, but it is, nonetheless, the basis of our relationship with God. God has not called men to supremacy. He has not anointed men as kings on this earth. Rather, He has commissioned us men to treat all other human beings with justice (fairness and equality) and mercy, and with a spirit of humility to recognize our dependence on Him and His incomprehensible love for all, especially the poor, the homeless, and the downtrodden.

Our security and value as men today is wrapped up in Him. It's true that He created man distinctly different from woman. Most men are content and even pleased with their maleness. Men's pleasure, however, comes not from being able to earn more, to dominate phys-ically, or to lord it over the opposite sex. Our pleasure comes from recognizing our uniqueness as males (children) of God, with individ-ual gifts and qualities imparted directly and specifically by Him.

Traditional thinking demands that men continually reestablish their manhood. Like a stag elk in charge of his harem of hinds, a man must demonstrate that he is still man enough to command re-spect. God's thinking frees us to be a male in God's image, with as much diversity as His creative imagination desires.

To be a man today is to recognize that some of the change that needs to take place in the world must begin with me. Men's and wom-en's roles are shifting, and as a result, my attitude may need adjusting.

But before we leave this chapter on our roles as providers, pro-tectors, and priests, let me suggest that these roles have not van-ished, but rather have been altered.

My role as the sole or primary financial provider for the home may be a thing of the past, but there is a very definite sense in which I am still needed to provide support that cannot be given by anyone else. As the man in the house, I need to give love, care, affirmation, and nurture. I need to give my wife the gift of myself and my time for communication. I have the privilege of providing that for her. It is possible for her to find listening partners elsewhere, but none can provide the inside understanding that I can.

I want to under-stand my wife's temperament and get to know her inti-mately. Only then can I provide the care and nurture that she, as an individ-ual, really needs. This is my unique, special opportunity to provide (give) and be needed (receive).

The new male needs desperately to come to grips with God's role for him as a man, rather than culture's expectations.

I can provide a role model for my children, my extended family, my church, and my community. Sadly, that aspect of the masculine role is often lacking. The world is a sorrier place because we have for too long assumed that our primary role as provider was materialistic. It takes more time, energy, and sacrifice to provide what is *really* needed, which is support and genuine caring.

> **My family may not need my physical protection in quite the same old ways. But what about an ever greater calling that might include protecting my wife's self-esteem?**

In a similar vein, my family may not need my physical protection in quite the same old ways, although that is not always true. But what about an even greater calling that might include protecting my wife's self-esteem? I have a unique opportunity to make my wife feel valuable as a woman. Nobody else can or should or should need to do that quite like I can.

I think that one of the greatest acts of protection I can give my entire family is to protect myself. I have seen far too many tragedies as a result of men not providing this basic protection. Most men would not think of canceling their life insurance policies to protect loved ones in the event of their death, but they don't protect themselves against infidelity. The earlier chapter titled "The Joy of Being Naked" gave some good ideas on getting started. The basic requirements are a willingness to do an honest self-evaluation and to establish open and honest communication with your spouse and with a cultivated, trusted friend. What better gift of love and affirmation could you give than allowing your family to see what high value you place on your relationship to them?

The role of priest likewise needs to be restored. This has nothing to do with the question of whether or not women are able to serve in ministry. The fact remains that our spouses and our families need to see us model the male attributes of priesthood. I have the opportunity to demonstrate and reflect Christ's selfless love. I can again affirm and show value for my wife by initiating time to read and pray together with her individually and with the family. I can further minister to her by fostering an overall atmosphere for true intimacy to develop. This is an intimacy that can exist only when *phileo* (friendship), *agape* (self-sacrificing), and *eros* (sexual) love are all present and working together.

Now my security and identity as a man is strengthened. I rest in God's steadfast love and acceptance, and I answer to His commission. My self-image is raised, and my wife's self-image is affirmed as well. My wife loves me for who I am. I am God's man.

Somehow I was brought up with the idea that I had to be as sexy as Tom Selleck, as smart as Henry Kissinger, as noble as Ralph Nader, as funny as Woody Allen, and as athletic as Mike Tyson.

My wife assures me that I am all of those things, but not necessarily in that order. She says that I'm as sexy as Woody Allen, as smart as Mike Tyson, as funny as Ralph Nader, as athletic as Henry Kissinger, and nothing at all like Tom Selleck, but she wouldn't trade me for any other man in the world. And I think she means it!

My security as a male should not depend upon my ability to be like other men or to outperform them. I feel secure in my wife's love, affirmation, and acceptance. That being the case, how much more secure a man should feel in Christ's love, affirmation, and acceptance! What could be more reaffirming than that?